ORIENTAL CLOISONNÉ

AND OTHER ENAMELS

Also by Arthur and Grace Chu

ORIENTAL ANTIQUES AND COLLECTIBLES: A GUIDE

ORIENTAL
CLOISONNÉ
AND OTHER ENAMELS

A Guide to
Collecting and Repairing

ARTHUR and GRACE CHU

CROWN PUBLISHERS, INC., NEW YORK

Copyright © 1975 by Arthur and Grace Chu

All rights reserved. No part of this book may be reproduced or utilized in any form or by any means, electronic or mechanical, including photocopying, recording, or by any information storage and retrieval system, without permission in writing from the publisher. Inquiries should be addressed to Crown Publishers, Inc., One Park Avenue, New York, N.Y. 10016

Printed in the United States of America

Published simultaneously in Canada by General Publishing Company Limited

Designed by Ruth Smerechniak

Library of Congress Cataloging in Publication Data

Chu, Arthur.
  Oriental cloisonné: a guide to collecting and repairing.

  Bibliography: p.
  Includes index.
  1. Cloisonné—China. 2. Cloisonné—Japan. 3. Cloisonné—Collectors and collecting.
I. Chu, Grace, joint author. II. Title.
NK5015.C45 1975   738.4   75-23441
ISBN: 0-517-523523

10 9 8 7 6 5 4

TO THE MEMORY OF OUR MOTHERS

Contents

Acknowledgments

We would like to thank those whose generosity and help not only were indispensable in the preparation of this book, but will always remain a cherished memory to us.

The editors of *Arts of Asia*, Mrs. Tuyet Nguyet and Mr. R. H. Leary, most graciously offered the use of their exclusive photos of the Inaba Cloisonné Factory. The *Arts of Asia* is our favorite magazine. Its articles are always timely and well researched. Located strategically in Hong Kong, the center of the collecting world of oriental art, the magazine reports on all the important international auctions and keeps its readers up to date on current market conditions as well as significant archaeological finds in the area. It is profusely illustrated with both color and black-and-white pictures. If we were allowed to choose only one word to describe the magazine, the word would have to be *beautiful*.

For many years, we have enjoyed the friendship of Jack Keller and Lewis Scott of Carmel, California. Owners of fine collections themselves, they literally halted their thriving business affairs at their two locations, whenever we appeared with our camera, to search for items needed for the illustration of this book. Likewise our friends of many years, the Hockabouts (Marvin, the genial antiquarian, and his charming wife, Wilma), would put away items from their salesroom until we, amateur photographers that we are, had produced satisfactory pictures.

We must not omit mentioning Mrs. Dorothy Adler Routh, who donated her splendid collection to Scripps College, Claremont, California. We are grateful to her for permission to reproduce pictures from her unedited, limited edition book *Asian Cloisonné Enamels*.

The name of Walter Chandoha is familiar to many of our readers. Author of many books, internationally known photographer whose pictures have appeared on the covers of over two hundred magazines, Mr. Chandoha is also an avid collector of cloisonné. Specimens of his collection that appear in this book, we are proud to add, were photographed by Mr. Chandoha himself.

To many others, collectors as well as museums, whose names appear either in the captions or in the text, we are grateful for their contributions.

As usual, we are reserving this space for a very special person, Kay Pinney, our editor and friend, whose counseling and encouragement made this undertaking possible. To her we want to say "To Sieh"—many, many thanks.

ORIENTAL
CLOISONNÉ
AND OTHER ENAMELS

Introduction

Suppose you have just bought a vase. It is decorated with a profusion of multicolored spring flowers, with birds perched on branches bursting out with tender leaves; or a dark wintry landscape with a flight of migrating cranes over it; or just a floral motif with an endless swerving, stylized yet graceful design, which you are instantly convinced has some deep symbolic meaning that has come down from time immemorial. Porcelain? Lacquer? No, even on the best of these the decorations would not be so sharply delineated. Could it be mosaic? You feel sure that a mosaic could never be so smooth-flowing. Perhaps it is inlay work of semiprecious stone. No, only inlays by the great Florentine artists are so seamless, you tell yourself as you close your eyes and run your fingers over the smooth surface.

You have in your hand a piece of oriental cloisonné. Even though neither

1

1. A bird on a prunus tree in full bloom, against a pastel pink ground, decorates this Japanese cloisonné vase. Height 9 inches.

the Chinese nor the Japanese craftsmen invented this art form—in fact, they learned it quite late and started making it without too much encouragement or enthusiasm from their rulers or the scholars who dictated the tastes of the time —yet, with their dexterous fingers and immense patience, they perfected it and gave the world a wealth of magnificent specimens. They also provided the moderately priced and still-plentiful collectible items on the antique market today. And it should be noted here that cloisonné articles are still being produced in China, Japan, and Taiwan perhaps with even greater excellence.

Because of the flamboyancy, the exuberance of the decoration, coupled with the intricacy of detail that characterizes these objects, many collectors of oriental art are fascinated by cloisonné. It is not a bad area for the would-be collector to start. Beginners will find cloisonné a very safe investment. The reason is simple. Most of the available pieces are products of the nineteenth or twentieth centuries. The value that comes from age—the all-important factor that determines the worth of most other art objects, such as porcelains, paintings, bronzes, and so on—is not often encountered here and can, therefore, be disregarded by the beginner. Specimens made during the Ming and early

2. Vase with white flying cranes against a jet black ground. Height 9 inches. Japanese.

3. A lotus scroll design surrounds the longevity character in black enamel on this Chinese cloisonné vase with an intense emerald green ground. Height 9 inches. Ca. 1920.

Ch'ing dynasties (roughly from the fifteenth century to the eighteenth century) are rare and are safely ensconced in museums.

Collectible cloisonné can easily be evaluated by (1) how much wire and enamel work there is; (2) how expertly, intricately, and artistically it is done; and (3), in rare cases, how valuable and important the base material is (gold or silver was occasionally used). Every bit of work is honestly done and honestly represented on the surface. No other art form—lacquer, porcelain, carved stone—can be mistaken for cloisonné, although the reverse could be true. (See Japanese Cloisonné, chapter 7.) If there are embellishments—for instance, reign marks—99 percent of them should be looked upon as decoration and nothing else.*

*Collectors should be particularly careful about paying a high price for pieces that are marked "Made in the Ching-t'ai Period," or "Made in the Great Ming Period," and believing they have acquired an authentic Ming piece. In a recent discussion with Jack Keller and Lewis Scott of Carmel, California, who specialize in fine oriental antiques and whose integrity and expertise are greatly respected by collectors, they told us they could not remember having acquired, during the last decade, any authentic specimen of the Hsüan-te or even Chia-ching or Wan-li periods. Sometimes, but very rarely, they had been fortunate enough to find one or two Ch'ien-lung pieces, but collectors snapped these up so quickly they hardly had time to enjoy them themselves.

There are very few books on the subject. Advanced collectors naturally are familiar with Sir Harry Garner's excellent and authoritative book, *Chinese and Japanese Cloisonné Enamels*. It is still by far the best book on cloisonné of the Ming and early Ch'ing periods. But for the beginner a reliable book of guidance is needed. This book is written to answer the need. The subjects discussed are, first, the nature of enamel and the manufacturing process; second, Chinese and Japanese cloisonné, with incidental reference to European and Islamic enamel work, the forerunner of Chinese and Japanese cloisonné; third, other enamel work such as champlevé and painted enamels; fourth, the marks, symbols, and motifs on oriental enamels. Finally, because most cloisonné pieces bear scars of damage, and because good repair and restoration services are scarce and exorbitantly priced when they are available, a sizable portion of this book will deal with the process of "do-it-yourself" repairs.

A price range of cloisonné is also provided. It must be stressed here, however, that this should not be interpreted as a strict price list, but only as a basis for comparison. Even in the time it takes to prepare a book, prices can fluctuate considerably. Therefore any price list is, at least to some degree, obsolete by the time the book appears, and may well become more so in a fairly short period. It is impossible to predict prices two years ahead of time, sometimes not even six months in advance. For instance, in 1973 prices for jade objects rose 600 to 1,000 percent. Needless to say, no expert—not even the most astute—could have foreseen this unprecedented leap. For yet another example: in the June 1974 sale of some of J. P. Morgan's household items, a collector paid $29,000 for a Ming statue that the auction house (no less a one than Sotheby Parke-Bernet) had appraised at $3,500—less than one-eighth the ultimate price it brought. It must be acknowledged here that such skilled appraisers know the market conditions far better than compilers of price lists. Hence, readers will be wise to treat all price lists as what they really are and not what they claim to be.

1

What Is Enamel?

THE ELEMENT THAT GIVES cloisonné objects their dazzling beauty is enamel. Enamel is glass. Perhaps we should qualify this by saying that it is a soft glass.

Again, like other types of glass, enamel in its pure and simple form is colorless and transparent. To give it color, various metallic oxides are added to it—for instance, copper for greens and turquoise, antimony for yellow, arsenic for white, manganese for the purples, cobalt for the blues; and, by a deoxidizing process, copper also produces various shades of red. Copper filings can be added to make a beautiful gold-flecked enamel used almost exclusively by the Japanese. To make these colors opaque, it is necessary to add tin oxide or even kaolin (clay) to the mixture. Degrees of opacity are achieved by varying the amount added.

Enamels are first made in large blocks or sticks of soft glass, which are then crushed and sifted before being sold to the workshops engaged in the art of enameling. Often they are in broken chunks when sold, and the enamelers themselves do the pulverizing and sifting.

Under a relatively low temperature of 850°C or less, powdered enamel will in minutes or even seconds melt into fluid form; when cooled, it will again become a solid mass. (Compare this, if you will, with the 1400°C and the continuous firing of several days needed to fuse the ingredients of porcelain.)

If the melted enamel is poured into a mold, it will, after hardening, permanently assume the shape of the mold. Imitation jewelry stones are often made this way.

To go a step further: if enamel paste (made by mixing pulverized enamel and water) is packed into little cells formed by metal wires or ribbons (as in cloisonné), or into cells carved or cast in solid metals (as in champlevé), and fired, the material will liquefy and tend to fill the spaces, and when it cools it forms a beautiful, multicolored design. This process is the basis of the art of enameling. Its products are almost unlimited: cloisonné, champlevé, basse-taille, repoussé, and painted enamels.

Before recorded history, man was entranced by the color and brilliance of natural stones. He believed that they had magical qualities that would keep away evil, ghosts, or diseases if worn on the person, besides serving the purpose of adornment. But natural stone is hard and extremely difficult to work with. Encasing stones in metal so that they could be worn presented still more difficulty. And to carve a design, even the simplest kind, was well-nigh impossible with man's first primitive tools.

Then came the discovery of glass, perhaps accidentally by early Mediterranean sailors when they made fires on the sandy beach with dried seaweed (potash or potassium carbonate) as part of the fuel. Glassmaking as an art had a magnificent history of its own in Egypt, Greece, Rome, and the Near East countries, but it is not within the scope of this book. With the invention of glass, however—or man-created precious and semiprecious stones—it became possible to design complicated decorative articles by filling metal encasements or bezels with glass paste of various colors and fusing them at relatively low temperatures. The products ranged from magnificent pieces for churches and palaces to small intimate pieces to be worn as jewelry.

Although glass artifacts have been found in Chinese tombs of the Middle and Late Chou period (approximately 600 B.C.), the oriental countries adopted glassmaking rather late and then only as a novelty. First of all, they had a prejudice against glass. Oriental people considered themselves possessors of a much superior art medium—they had porcelain. Oriental art is based on dynamic lines and on shapes and forms that display those lines to advantage. Porcelain can be modeled sculpturally to achieve this purpose much better than glass (although the Chinese did experiment with carving the chunks of glass exported by Roman and Byzantine dealers). Also, glass was regarded as

4. Chinese vase with heavy hammered copper base has lotus scrolls on the body and cloud patterns on the neck. The green background is so dark it is almost black. Late seventeenth or early eighteenth century; height 10 inches.

5. Champlevé water dropper. Early nineteenth century; Japanese. The water dropper, an indispensable item for the scholar's desk, is made in many fanciful shapes and forms—animals, fruits, fish, and so on. It holds a small amount of water that is poured, drops at a time, onto the ink stone. The ink stick is then rubbed vigorously on the stone to produce the ink. *Keller & Scott, Carmel, California*

only a substitute for or imitation of better things, such as jade, coral, lapis. The proof is not far to seek. All the glasswares known as Peking glass were meant to be imitations of one kind of semiprecious stone or another. This fact offers one explanation of why the oriental countries developed the art of enameling rather late. It is quite certain that they learned the techniques from the West and through the Middle East. But they surpassed their teachers and during the nineteenth and twentieth centuries monopolized the export market with tremendous quantities of beautiful cloisonné items—vases, jars, bowls, cups, ashtrays, napkin rings. Because the aim of Chinese glass is to imitate natural stones, it was at first opaque. When it appeared as enamels in cloisonné work, they too were opaque, even though sometimes semiopaque enamels were used. Modern Japanese cloisonné, however, is distinguished by the use of a good deal of transparent and translucent enamel. The differences between Chinese and Japanese cloisonné will be dealt with in later chapters.

2

What Is Cloisonné?

IN SPITE OF THE RISK of being needlessly repetitious, there is no better way to define the term than to join all the former writers on the subject and say that the word cloisonné comes from the French word *cloison*, which means "cell" or the "walls that form the cell." An art object or design consisting of cells filled with variously colored enamels separated from one another by metal ribbons or wires soldered or glued onto a suitable base is called a cloisonné enamel.

The wire walls serve two functions: aesthetic and structural. Enamels, when fired, tend to run into one another, and not only would the delineation of the design be destroyed without some device for separating the colors, but the mixture of different enamel colors would be likely to result in unpleasant and muddy tones. The walls eliminate this problem by providing crisp, clear-cut outlines. A fired enamel and its metal base do not make a strong and permanent union; the difference between the enamel and the metal, in rate of expansion and contraction, creates a stress between them. As time passes, the enamel (the weaker of the two) will tend to crack and pop off. Therefore the wires also serve a structural purpose—as anchors for the enamels; they provide strength by sharing and breaking up the stresses.

Some metals are more suitable than others for the base and for the wires that contain the enamels. They do not melt at the temperature of 850°C at which all enamels fuse. The metals must also be reasonably pliable so that they can be drawn or hammered into wire or shaped into the desired form for a bowl, plate, or vase. They should also have an attractive color and not be subject to easy oxidation. For all these reasons, gold and its various alloys would be the most suitable. But gold and even silver have always been expensive, and in the early days only the emperor or the very rich could afford pieces made with such costly materials. Next in suitability, but far less expensive, are copper and its alloys of bronze and brass. These were not costly, and so were particularly suitable where a large quantity of metal had to be employed for large specimens.

The body (or base) is either cast or hammered from sheets of metal into the desired forms, often at the same workshop that makes the cloisonné. Bases are also made at metal factories that specialize in supplying cloisonné workshops. The designs are outlined on the metal base, and the wires cut and soldered to the base following the designated outlines. The use of solder during the early days (that is, the Ming dynasty) produced some unpleasant effects. With its low melting point, solder would often bubble to the surface during the firing, discoloring the enamels. In later times the wires were merely glued onto the base. The glue would burn away during the firing without affecting the enamels.

When the wires have been placed properly over the object, the enamels are wet-charged into the cells or spaces. The enamels are already in powder form, well ground and sifted and mixed with water, forming a sort of glass paste. This paste is lifted with a brush or tiny spatula bit by bit to fill the cells.

After the filling is done, the piece is fired in a kiln or oven for a few minutes until the glass paste fuses or melts. Then it is taken out and cooled in a protected area. The enamel in each cell will have shrunk to two-thirds its original size, but the level of the fused enamel will be slightly higher along the wires and lowest at the center of each cell. The cells are now filled again. This process may have to be repeated several times for a heavy piece of exceptional quality. When the enamel level is slightly above the wires, the filling and firing process is complete.

The next steps are grinding and polishing. On flat pieces, grinding is done with a stone. On a round piece such as a vase, the lathe will be used. This process is no different from any type of lapidary work. First the enamels are smoothly ground down to the level of the wires; then the piece is polished to a high gloss. Chinese cloisonnés, however, were often left in a state of semigloss, a rather satiny finish. Also, on Chinese cloisonné the wires and other exposed metal parts such as the lip and foot ring were gilded. This was easy to do because the enamels, by their very nature, do not take on the gilding. As a rule, Japanese cloisonné is not often gilded.

During the 1920s and 1930s, the Chinese exported sets of five to seven small vases contained in a glass-covered box, which show the different stages of cloisonné manufacture. Usually these included vases (1) with only the wires attached; (2) after the first firing; (3) after the second firing; (4) after grinding; (5) after polishing; and (6) after gilding. Although these sets have no artistic value, they are good illustrations of the manufacturing process. Now and then one can still be bought at an antique shop.

Perhaps it is well to mention here that the Chinese made an openwork form of cloisonné on which the enamel was applied to the design only, and the background was left unfilled but gilded. The unsatisfactory term "openwork" is adopted here over other equally unsatisfactory ones to describe this technique of breaking up the surface and creating a more interesting relief effect.

Collectors usually consider Chinese and Japanese cloisonnés in a class by themselves. They are unique because not only do the designs and motifs, shapes and forms, impart an oriental feeling, but also they are the purest form of the cloisonné technique. Examples from the West are very different. They often combine two or three techniques in one piece—champlevé, repoussé, or high relief in cast bronze or gold, with cloisonné and even jewel-encrusted embellishment; sometimes the cloisonné is only a small part of the total. The ancient European work was almost always on plaques or flat slabs to be attached to doors or walls, or on minute pieces inserted in frames or put on vessels. These have a mosaic quality because of their uneven surface. Large pieces in the round are rare among European cloisonnés, but it is not uncommon to see oriental specimens six to eight feet tall.

6. Small tray; Chinese. The center panel is regular cloisonné but the outer ring is "openwork." The lotus scrolls are filled with enamels; the background is gilded copper. Diameter 3½ inches. Ca. 1920.

7. Chinese cloisonné Fo dog, perhaps the largest cloisonné in existence. Height 7 feet 9½
inches. Late seventeenth or early eighteenth century. *The University Museum, University of
Pennsylvania. Philadelphia*

Today it is increasingly popular to collect oriental cloisonné because it is more available, more reasonably priced, and more decorative than many other oriental art objects. And if a collector does not limit himself entirely to collecting the antique type (loosely, pieces over 100 years old), there are new pieces available coming from China, Japan, and Taiwan. Their quality is kept to the exacting standards set by tradition. One need not apologize for including some modern pieces in a collection—in a few years the difference will scarcely be noticeable.

Unlike that of porcelain, cloisonné art is rather limited in its expression. Its attractiveness lies in its intricate design, the impact on our senses of its ornate beauty and brilliantly colored enamels.

We have mentioned that enamel is glass, and the enamel of cloisonné can be cleaned just as glass is. Use soap and water to remove the dust and fumes accumulated through the years and bring back the beauty and brilliance. Damage, of course, makes even the most precious specimen of cloisonné something of an eyesore, and if it is left unrepaired, the copper will oxidize and the enamels will drop off. Proper repairs should be made as soon as possible to avoid further deterioration. The reader can easily follow the techniques explained in the last chapter of this book to achieve satisfactory results.

3

Champlevé, Painted Enamel, Repoussé, Basse-Taille

ANOTHER TYPE OF ENAMEL WORK that bears great similarity to cloisonné is champlevé, but it has not been as popular as cloisonné in the oriental countries. The technique was mastered in Europe in about the ninth century. The massive pieces on display in museums around the world are beautiful in their extravagance of color and added use of jewels. Although the method originated in Europe, the Japanese manufactured and exported a great number of massive, ornate pieces of champlevé during the early 1900s. Because they are not as fragile as cloisonné, many of them are in surprisingly good condition; they are still readily found on the market today.

Champlevé pieces are heavy and sturdy because they were usually cast from bronze, then smoothly polished and lacquered so that they have an antique look. The enamels were often limited to the archaistic colors—blue, red, white,

8. Bronze vase with a band of enamel decoration. Height 10 inches. Ca. 1900. Japanese champlevé.

9. Bronze pan with stylized lotus scroll champlevé decoration around the rim. Diameter 12 inches. Ca. 1900. Japanese.

10. Ku-shaped Japanese bronze vase. The paulownia flowers and leaves in champlevé enamels were appliquéd to the bronze body. Height 12 inches. Ca. 1900.

11. Base of the vase in Ill. 10. Strangely, it carries a Wan-li reign mark of the Chinese Ming dynasty. Japanese champlevé pieces so marked date from around 1900.

brown. Most specimens do not have allover decoration, but only bands of typically archaistic designs. Some of the enameled decorations are appliquéd; in other words, individually enameled champlevé pieces are soldered onto the body to form the decoration.

Sometimes it is difficult for the beginner to distinguish between cloisonné and champlevé. (See Color Plate 10.) Both have enamels enclosed in cells formed by metallic borders. The main difference is that the walls in cloisonné are formed by wires or ribbons soldered or glued to the metal body, whereas in champlevé the cells are formed by casting, chiseling, or etching. For this reason, the object itself has to be thick and heavy, of cast bronze or brass; the body of modern cloisonné, by contrast, is hammered out of copper sheets and is much thinner and lighter. There is no need to explain how the gouging is done, but perhaps a word needs to be said about the relatively recent method of etching. First, a heavy waxy material is used to cover and protect the parts that are not to be filled with enamel. Next, the piece is immersed in acid to dissolve out the metal according to the planned design. When the proper depth has been reached, the piece is taken out of the acid, rinsed thoroughly, and made ready for the enamel. Sometimes additional hand-chiseling work is needed to complete the design for a really fine piece.

To distinguish a piece of cloisonné from a piece of champlevé, it is necessary to see if the metal elements enclosing the cells are individually placed (cloisonné) or a part of the body itself (champlevé). That is, are the edges or ends of a design (an arabesque, for instance) actually an extension of the body metal? Close examination will reveal places where the "design dividers" and the body of the object are clearly one piece of metal (champlevé). It is also helpful to remember that as a rule champlevé has a heavier body, with thicker and often uneven dividing walls, than cloisonné. Large, heavy pieces with only decorative enameled bands are almost invariably champlevé rather than cloisonné. It is well said that cloisonné is the art of the goldsmith and champlevé that of the coppersmith.

Many small items, such as buttons, earrings, place-card holders, finger rings, and club emblems, are machine-stamped to create the designs. The cells are then filled with a thin layer of enamel. These items are related more nearly to champlevé than to any other type of enamel work.

12. Champlevé incense burner with removable saddle lid. Height 3 inches; length 5 inches. Marked "Nippon."

13. Place-card holder decorated with a snowy scene that has Mount Fuji in the background. The design is machine stamped and the enamels thinly applied. A type of Japanese champlevé.

14. A type of Japanese champlevé with machine-stamped design. The enamel was ground and polished and the metal part silver gilded. Ca. 1960.

15. Shank-type buttons have a machine-stamped design of double gourds on vines surrounding the longevity character. Chinese champlevé.

16. The Flying Tiger emerging from a victory V, badge of the first American Volunteer Group (General Chennault's famed Flying Tigers), which drove the Japanese airplanes from the Chinese sky during World War II. But this machine-stamped badge was made in the United States and designed by one of the most famous Hollywood cartoonists. (Need we tell you his name?) A type of champlevé.

PAINTED ENAMELS

The fact seems to have been established that cloisonné was introduced to the Orient from the Islamic countries during the thirteenth and/or fourteenth centuries. Toward the beginning of the eighteenth century another technique, enamel painting, was introduced into China from France. This process begins by putting a primary coating of white opaque enamel on a metal body (usually copper, although gold or silver was sometimes used). Then a theme or design and sometimes a background of color are painted over the white, much as overglaze enameling is done on porcelain. For this reason, the Chinese call painted enamels "foreign porcelain." The technique immediately became popular with Chinese artisans because it gave them an opportunity to exercise their delicate brush-painting skills. Therefore, the most important standard in judging a piece of painted enamel is how good the painting or artwork is.

In Canton, a thriving industry soon grew up around the making and exporting of painted enamels. Hence we have the terms "Canton enamels" and "Peking enamels." Specifically, the second term refers to the more refined items first produced in the emperor's workshops and then in private factories around Peking, where Western motifs and subjects were often used. Since painted enamels were considered "foreign porcelain," imaginative craftsmen soon found them a suitable medium for irrelevancies, humor, and satire. Foreigners were often the subject of caricature on these pieces.

This type of enamel work was practiced almost exclusively by the Chinese. The Japanese do not seem to have engaged in it, certainly not to the extent that it became a characteristic product of Japan. (See Color Plate 15.)

17. Chinese painted-enamel potiche decorated with a pheasant on a rock and a peony flower. The painting is of superb quality; background is robin's-egg blue. Height approx. 20 inches. Ca. 1900. *Dr. and Mrs. Marvin Hockabout Collection*

18. Reverse side of the potiche shown in Ill. 17, with butterfly and tree peony.

19. Center panel of this Chinese painted-enamel plate depicts the famous story of Su Wu, who as a young man was sent as ambassador to a barbaric border nation by the Chinese emperor, detained there as a hostage, and made to attend a flock of sheep. For eighteen years, Su's loyalty never changed. When he was released by the barbarians, who finally had realized they could not change him, his hair and beard had turned completely white. Su has since then served as a symbol of constancy and loyalty. This painting is of excellent quality. Diameter approx. 10 inches. *Keller & Scott, Carmel, California*

20. Chinese painted-enamel plate decorated with thunder pattern on the border and an intricate and delicate floral pattern in pastel colors on a white background. Diameter 8 inches.

21. The dragon on this Chinese enamel bowl is painted against a pink background. Diameter approx. 9 inches. *Dr. and Mrs. Marvin Hockabout Collection*

22. Stem dish of Chinese painted-enamel with design of plum blossoms and bamboo over a cracked-ice ground of purplish blue. Diameter 7 inches.

23. Top view of the dish shown in Ill. 22.

24. Tray in the shape of a leaf is decorated with a bird and floral design on pink ground. Chinese painted enamel.

25. Chinese painted-enamel box with fair figure painting; however, the colors are good. The border is bright blue with orange flowers. Length 6 inches; width 3 inches; depth 2½ inches.

26. Box with poor figure painting in panels on all four sides and the top. Background is an unusual deep purple red color. Chinese painted enamel.

27. A boat-shaped Chinese painted-enamel dish—both inside and upright view. (Actually, it is the shape of ingots of Chinese gold or silver bullion.)

28. Large oblong tray of Chinese painted enamel with floral design over a purple ground. The center panel shows a garden scene with two young children and an old man with a peach in his hand. The painting is only fair.

29. Large stack dishes (containers for food or sweetmeats) of Chinese painted enamel. Each dish bears a different scene depicting Chinese life. Diameter 8 inches; height of each tray 2 inches. Ca. 1920.

30. Round Chinese painted-enamel box with floral design on a royal blue background. The shape is the only thing that is commendable about this piece. The enamels were carelessly applied and the painting is very poor.

31. Top view of the box in Ill. 30.

32. Small bowl of Chinese painted enamel with floral design in deep harmonious colors. The design is raised in low relief and outlined with gold. Diameter 3½ inches.

33A. Hexagonal bowl, Chinese painted enamel; each side is decorated with the double gourd and other Chinese fruits on a yellow ground.

33B. Another example of beauty of line in the shape and design of a decorative Chinese painted-enamel bowl. The enamels are light blue and pink.

34. Originally a part of the elaborate decoration on a lantern; now made into the pendant of a necklace. Chinese painted enamel—dark blue black on cobalt background. Length 4 inches; width 2½ inches.

35. Chinese painted-enamel caddy for a package of cigarettes and a matchbox. The miniature paintings are very fine.

36. Serving plate of Chinese painted enamel with good landscape painting on a white ground. Diameter 8 inches.

REPOUSSÉ

Repoussé is metal stamped or pressed into a design from the underside of an article, in either high or low relief. After enamel is applied, the relief remains. Sometimes a high relief motif is also enameled; sometimes (as on many Chinese bronze items) it is only the background of the design that is enameled, leaving the bronze relief design showing.

BASSE-TAILLE

Basse-taille refers to the technique of submerging a metal piece that was carved or stamped with a relief design under a heavy coat of transparent or translucent enamel, leaving the surface of the item entirely level.

Both repoussé and basse-taille are at their best when the base metal is gold, silver, or gilded copper. A silver or gold foil pressed firmly over the base metal design will give the same effect. The enamels, of course, must be of the transparent or translucent kind. The result is often a creation of the utmost delicacy and subtlety.

37. Chinese cylinder-shaped box of repoussé work partly covered with opaque enamels, with the bronze relief showing. Center panel is of two scholars playing chess. The borders at top and bottom depict various traditional symbols. Height 4 inches; diameter 2½ inches.

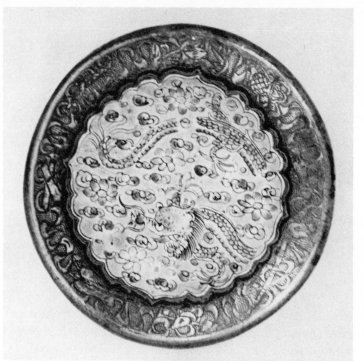

38. Center medallion of this tray is decorated in painted enamels depicting a dragon among clouds; pastel colors on a white ground. The outer ring shows the symbols of the eight Taoist immortals in repoussé work. Diameter 4½ inches. Chinese.

39. Bronze seal and ink box with background enameled in opaque white. The repoussé flowers and leaves stand out sharply. Chinese.

40. Small tray with floral design in delicate translucent enamels in bright pastel colors over a silvered ground; actual size. Repoussé work is in low relief. Chinese.

41. Repoussé box and two trays decorated with pastel enamels over silver gilding. The heavy overlay of transparent enamel creates a basse-taille effect. Length 5 inches; width 3½ inches; depth 2½ inches. Chinese.

42. Tray with swerving and reticulated design surrounding the "longevity" character is decorated with thin translucent blue and purple enamels over an incised silvered ground. Size, 4½ inches square. Chinese.

43. Heavy-duty tray decorated with peaches on a branch in low-relief repoussé. The enamels are translucent pastels over silver gilding. The entire plate is covered with a thick clear enamel giving a basse-taille effect. Diameter 8 inches. Chinese.

44. Chinese covered box in the shape of a squash has incised decoration. The silvered base is covered by a translucent yellow gold enamel, with patches of green and green leaves. Diameter 7½ inches. Ca. 1920.

45. Miniature vessel in the form of archaic bronze I, low relief repoussé, and covered by translucent pastel enamels over a silvered base. This is an upright view. Chinese.

46. Inside view of the piece shown in Ill. 45. Dragon and thundercloud appear against a robin's-egg blue ground.

47. High relief repoussé caddy (*top view*) with curved handle; done in translucent enamels over a silvered base. The design is a copy of an archaic painting. Chinese.

48. Chinese jar with "openwork" type of cloisonné and gold gilding. The wires are twisted like a rope or thread. Only the important elements are filled with translucent enamels. This technique is more often seen on small jewelry items. It is a direct imitation of European twisted-wire finish.

49. Chatelaine of high-quality bronze with twisted wires in the European mode. The water carrier, arrow-pierced heart, four-leaf clover, and jointed fish are finished with transparent colored enamels. Chinese.

50. Chinese seal box of the "openwork" cloisonné type. Silver gilding with translucent enamels fills the important parts of the design. The wires are plain rather than twisted.

To complete this short discussion of the art of enameling, it is necessary to make at least a brief mention of several kinds of European enamels that reached a high degree of perfection both in technique and in their artistic quality during the Renaissance. Painters in enamel developed the use of chiaroscuro to a high level. They wanted to imitate the glorious paintings of the time (and actually copied many) and were able to do so by careful handling of the enamels, firing each shading as it was added. They also practiced a very early niello technique, a rather simple one in which a deeply engraved line is filled with a grayish-black metallic substance. This produces an outline like a drawing.

Another technique, grisaille, consisted of accenting high relief repoussé by the use of white over black enamel, firing after each application, to create varying shades of gray. These pieces are almost indistinguishable from cameos carved from black and white shell.

But to try to trace the ultimate origin of the art of enameling would only leave the reader needlessly frustrated. Shrouded by speculation, elusive as the Loch Ness Monster, the true facts perhaps will never be known. As one of our collector friends is fond of reciting at the end of his lectures on the subject:

> *Egyptians, Persians, Syrians,*
> *Byzantians, Mesopotamians, and Mergovingians;*
> *Mycenaeans, Carolingians, and Sarmations,*
> *Who were the first to make cloisonné and champlevé?*
> *And who gave enamel to the whole wide world*
> *The Romans, the Celts, or the Islams?*
> *Historians conjecture much, but cannot say*
> *Who first made cloisonné and champlevé.*

Although his rhyming efforts do not exactly run "trippingly on the tongue," we must admit that there is a good deal of truth in his jingle.

4

Chinese
Cloisonné —
The Ming Period

CHINESE POETS OFTEN SING with ecstasy of the beauty of porcelain. Tu Fu (712-770), one of the greatest poets, says:

> *The porcelain of Ta-yi is light and yet strong.*
> *It rings with a melancholy jade note,*
> *The fine white bowls surpass hoarfrost and snow.*

Another praises Yüeh ware, an early celadon:

> *The misty scenery of the late autumn appears when Yüeh kilns*
>   *are thrown open;*
> *The thousand peaks have been robbed of their color for the*
>   *decoration of the bowls.*

Still another describes porcelain as being

Like ancient moss-grown bronze mirrors, lying upon the mat;
Like tender lotus leaves, full of dew, floating beside the river.

What did the Chinese literary men, the dictators of taste, think of cloisonné? Ts'ao Chao (the author of *Ko Ku Yao Lun*), who lived in the fourteenth century and was considered one of the greatest connoisseurs, had this to say: "I have seen such things as incense burners, flower vases, boxes, and cups. They are fit for use in women's boudoirs, and are quite inappropriate for companionship with the scholar in his studio. It [cloisonné] is also called 'devil country ware.' "

From the above statements, it is apparent that in spite of the magnificent specimens produced by the Chinese, to the scholar-connoisseurs the only function of cloisonné was to satisfy the female fancy for the gaudy. (Have men always been chauvinistic?) Worse still, it originated from "devil country" or foreign soil.

Nonetheless, in spite of the discouraging first reception given cloisonné by the Chinese and also the Japanese, whose criteria generally paralleled those of the Chinese, cloisonné workers doggedly carried on and improved their techniques steadily. By the time of the Emperor K'ang-hsi (1662-1722), one of the palace workshops (alongside those producing native crafts for palace use) was devoted to the making of cloisonné.

Compared to the other arts and crafts of China, her cloisonné has had a relatively short history. Even though it has been claimed that the Chinese first made cloisonné as early as the T'ang dynasty (A.D. 618-907), there is little proof of the fact. The only evidence offered is the twelve-pointed cloisonné mirror preserved at Sho-so-in* in Nara, Japan. This is undated, and there is no record as to when it was deposited at the museum. Conjectures about its origin vary from T'ang Chinese to seventeenth-century Japanese. Recent research, however, has established the fact that the Chinese did use enamels as a sort of champlevé decoration on their ceremonial bronzes as early as the later part of the Chou dynasty (1122-221 B.C.).

As a practical matter, it is safer to move the date down to the Yüan (Mongol) dynasty (A.D. 1277-1368). In the first place, there are more reliable written records to follow. For instance, in a rare poem—rare because the author was willing to speak quite favorably of this new art form and thus ran the risk of being ridiculed by his fellow literary men and scholars—Wu Yüan-ying said that it was introduced into China from Persia, and new in his lifetime. (Wu died in 1326.) Second, history tends to bear this out. The Mongols, after

*Sho-so-in is a depository for the treasures of the Emperor Shomu, who died in A.D. 756. However, many other items were also deposited at much later dates. The controversy concerning the cloisonné enameled mirror, variously believed to be of Chinese T'ang dynasty origin or early Japanese make, is still not settled.

having subdued China, went on to conquer the world and establish a gigantic empire over most of Asia and the adjacent lands. Many of these countries were well advanced in the cloisonné technique. Among the prisoners taken back, there would surely have been craftsmen skilled in this art, and they would have been expected to make the most beautiful specimens to please and gain favor from their conquerors.

Further proof comes from the names the Chinese first gave this new ware. It was called "ta-shih" ware and "kuei-kuo" ware. "Ta-shih" refers to the land of Arabia, and "kuei-kuo" carries the uncomplimentary connotation of "devil's country." These names definitely establish its non-Chinese origin.

The Yüan or Mongol dynasty, which did not care about the artistic achievements of China, did not last long. The Ming dynasty that overthrew and succeeded it was again Chinese and naturally restored and fostered the traditional values, both ethical and artistic.

As has already been mentioned, prominent connoisseurs did not consider these "gaudy" cloisonné objects as fit companions for a scholar-gentleman in his study. A scholar-gentleman, in the Chinese sense, was a man of refinement and an arbiter of artistic taste. Hence, it is clear that, during the Ming dynasty, cloisonné did not have status as an art form. It was much below jade, porcelain, bamboo, and wood carvings, all of which the scholar could unashamedly display or fondle in his study. Still, it was during that dynasty, as early as the reign of Hsüan-te (1426-1435), that the Chinese produced the most magnificent pieces of cloisonné. No doubt by that time it had achieved some small degree of popularity, enough to create a demand for such a colorful novelty.

The Chinese term for cloisonné is Ching-t'ai lan—literally "the blue of the Emperor Ching-t'ai"—so it can be said that cloisonné is named after one of the Ming emperors. (Another less colorful name for the ware is translated as "working with wires," or "the manipulation of wires.") The blue, a clear bright turquoise, was often used as a background—in contrast to the other Ming enamels: the dark green, the deep purplish or sometimes grayish cobalt blue, the red, yellow, and white.

Why was cloisonné named after Emperor Ching-t'ai? There is no record of his being the promoter or patron of this particular art. One of his predecessors, the Emperor Yung-lo, sent fleets to visit all the South Sea countries under the command of his very capable eunuch Cheng Ho, a man of the Moslem faith. They even reached the shores of Africa, and this success resulted in exchanges of technology. But Ching-t'ai—there is no record of his having had anything to do with cloisonné. In fact, there is no record of his achieving anything in the field of Chinese art. However, the story of how he came to the throne may be of interest.

During his time, a quarrel arose between the Ming Chinese and the Mongols, who had been driven out of China proper by the founding Ming emperors and were now raiding and skirmishing along the border. The young emperor was talked into personally leading an army to punish the Mongols, by his favorite eunuch, who, knowing nothing about military arts, yet assumed command. The large but ill-trained army moved north on an auspicious day selected by astrologers, without competent commanders, without strategy. The expedition was to provide the emperor with an outing. As they progressed, with banners, carriages, and all the provisions fit for an emperor, they made very little contact with the enemy, but the alert Mongol horsemen were just waiting for their chance. When boredom set in, as the expedition became routine and lost its excitement, the eunuch contrived—for diversion—to induce the emperor to visit his estate for a few days. In grandeur it was comparable to the palaces in Peking. However, because of the size of the royal entourage, the eunuch was afraid that the crops in the fields he owned would be trampled by the party. He mapped a circuitous route, and this took the procession close to the enemy. The Mongols ambushed the party, routing the ill-trained and ill-disciplined army and capturing the emperor, whom the Mongol chief thereafter held as hostage, in order to blackmail the Ming Chinese.

Before the emperor left on this ill-fated expedition, he had appointed his brother Ching-t'ai as the regent. After the disaster, the state council asked Ching-t'ai to ascend the throne as ruler, and assigned to the captured emperor the exalted title of Grand Emperor (Emperor emeritus). This was not only a wise—but perhaps the only—course to follow: that is, depriving the Mongols of the means of blackmailing the Ming Chinese. The annals of the Ming dynasty are besmirched with the names of several briefly reigning, indolent, deplorable rulers, but Ching-t'ai was not one of them. He secured China's borders against the Mongols and eventually managed to get his captive brother released. When the "Grand Emperor" returned to the palace, he was greatly honored and respected, but he did not attempt to reclaim the throne. He had subjected the country to a period of danger and the threat of enemy extortion, whereas his brother Ching-t'ai was a diligent and good ruler who managed the nation's affairs without fault. There was no valid reason for the Grand Emperor's restoration.

But a conspiracy was brewing secretly. One day when Ching-t'ai was ill, an early-morning coup d'état carried out by a small faction restored the captive emperor to the throne, to the great dismay of the nation. This coup was one of the strangest incidents of the Ming dynasty. After the overthrow of Ching-t'ai, a story manufactured by the conspirators claimed that over the tent where the formerly captive emperor had slept while he was held by the Mongols, a five-clawed golden dragon had been seen circling every night, to protect its occupant. This frightened the Mongol chief and made him realize that his captive was the one and only true "Son of Heaven" and that he was courting disaster by thwarting the will of Heaven. He therefore decided to return the captive emperor. Actually, it was Ching-t'ai's skilled handling of the border defenses that made the Mongol chief realize he had nothing to gain by holding onto his hostage and caused him to seek a reconciliation.

Following the coup, vengeance seemed to be heaped upon poor Ching-t'ai.

When he died not long afterward, he was refused the burial in the imperial mausoleum to which he was entitled, and later he was given the humiliating posthumous title of "substitute emperor." Thus ended the sad and bitter story of Ching-t'ai. Was he poisoned? The official history of the Ming dynasty is studiously abbreviated and vague.

It was not known, and perhaps never will be, why cloisonné was named after the luckless Ching-t'ai. Perhaps it was the common people's way of expressing their sympathy for him and their fond memory of a ruler unjustly overthrown and unfairly treated. Chinese craftsmen often deify a dead person by naming him as guardian spirit, and cloisonné, a new craft just introduced into China, still needed a guardian spirit. The dethroned emperor might have been, at the moment, the only appropriate and available candidate. The essence of deification is often the fact that the person so elevated was grossly wronged during his lifetime, and public sentiment demanded something be done to right matters. Ironically, Ching-t'ai, emperor by accident, became better known to posterity than many other Ming monarchs through another accident—a minor art form originating in foreign lands and considered as unfit for the refined tastes of the scholar-gentlemen. To be sure, this is mostly speculation.

Because pieces carrying the Ching-t'ai reign mark are traditionally highly valued and much sought after by collectors, many faked pieces came into being during subsequent periods—the seventeenth century or later, when the name "Ching-t'ai lan" for cloisonné was in common use and the Ching-t'ai myth had become well established.* Therefore the age of early Chinese cloisonné objects can be determined only by close examination of the style of the decoration, the enamels, and the kind of metal alloy of which the body and wires were made.

No doubt genuine Ching-t'ai specimens do exist. The new industry was carried on by small workshops or by families, perhaps of the Mohammedan faith. Unlike porcelain, cloisonné did not enjoy imperial patronage nor was it subject to control. The Emperor Hsüan-te ruled nine years (1426-1435) and Ching-t'ai seven years (1450-1457)—there was a gap of only fifteen years between them. There is no reason to suppose that there should have been any great change in its manufacture. There are many genuine pieces of Hsüan-te cloisonné in existence today, and there is absolutely no reason why the cloisonné industry should have stopped production during the reign of Ching-t'ai and resumed only after his death. There is the further possibility that since cloisonné did not attract much attention before the Wan-li reign (1573-1620) and did not enjoy imperial patronage until the K'ang-hsi period (1662-1722), most of the early Ming pieces were not marked at all, and, when they were, the marks were often apocryphal. The same question of authenticity can and

---

*Sir Harry Garner, *Chinese and Japanese Cloisonné Enamels*, Chapter 6. R. H. Leary, "Cloisonné: The Ching T'ai Myth," *Arts of Asia*, Vol. 5, No. 1.

perhaps should be raised about those specimens with the Hsüan-te mark. We know only too well that the Hsüan-te mark has been used indiscriminately on all Chinese bronzes made since that reign. In the case of cloisonné, a reign mark can be incised or the whole bottom replaced in a matter of minutes.

Vintage Ming cloisonné objects are scarce—much scarcer than Ming porcelain, as might be expected—because (as we have already implied) the resources and the effort devoted to cloisonné production, compared to those afforded the porcelain industry, were mere drops in the bucket. Most existing pieces are in museums. When a piece does come on the market, the price can be astronomical. It is a thrilling experience to study the few early Ming specimens that some museums have acquired either through donations or farsighted purchase. The bodies are heavy cast bronze with handwrought bronze wires placed with extreme care, but sometimes betraying the unsure workmanship of a new craft. The most popular design is the gracefully swerving lotus scroll, a feature popularized by the blue and white Ming porcelain. Indeed, there are signs of communication and mutual influence between the two art media. For instance, it was at this time that the porcelain industry borrowed the cloisonné technique (*fa-hua*) and began using clay strips to form cells to prevent the various colored glazes from running into one another. Most cloisonné specimens still retain their original gilding; the few simple and unassuming enamel colors, against the typically cheerful, bright turquoise background, and the uncomplicated designs contribute to their charm. In spite of their ornate look, they exhibit the virtues of strength and dignity.

The early Ming period or the fifteenth century is indeed the golden age of Chinese cloisonné. Changes, though slight and gradual, occurred during the middle and late Ming period—that is, the next two and a half centuries. Enamel colors increased in variety, though their quality did not necessarily improve. Designs became more open. This necessitated the use of scrollwork, which was often irrelevant and certainly contributed nothing aesthetically, for the support of the enamels. In the manufacture of the bodies, hammered copper sheet took the place of cast bronze, but the pieces were fitted with bronze neck and foot rings. Wires remained bronze throughout the Ming dynasty. This imparts a pleasing golden tone to the exposed metal of Ming cloisonné even after the gilding has worn off. (For Ming specimens, see Color Plates 1 and 2. The Ching-t'ai dating is controversial. However, we defer to the opinion of the Palace Museum until such time as a consensus among scholars can be reached.)

It is not our purpose to dwell in minute detail on all the aspects of Ming cloisonné, since this book is written for collectors who may not be in a position to spend hundreds of thousands of dollars on their hobby. For those who want to make further studies of early Chinese cloisonné, we recommend the scholarly work of Sir Harry Garner, *Chinese and Japanese Cloisonné Enamels*. Its treatment of Ming and early Ch'ing cloisonné can hardly be improved upon.

5

Transition and
the Establishment
of the Ch'ing Style

THROUGH A SERIES OF INDOLENT RULERS and their misrule, the Ming dynasty came to an end. The immediate cause was the rising of roving bandits, largely famine-stricken peasants from all over the country. Unable to suppress the bandits, the Ming generals invited the Manchus to come inside the Great Wall to help do the job. The Manchus refused to leave—instead, they set up their own dynasty, the Ch'ing.

The Ming dynasty officially ended in A.D. 1644. But the Ming Chinese, hating another foreign rule (the Manchus, like the Mongols, were at that time considered to be a tribal nation, not part of China proper), kept setting up one ruler after another as they fled south with the Manchus in busy pursuit. Next came the revolt of the Chinese generals who had initially enlisted the Manchus' help and had cooperated with the conquerors in exchange for favors.

38

51. Goblet with lotus scroll decor on turquoise ground. Seventeenth century. Height 11 inches.

Large-scale fighting spread over several provinces and destroyed the famous porcelain manufacturing center at Ching-te-chen. It was eventually put down by K'ang-hsi, the second ruler of the Manchu period. K'ang-hsi was an unusually brilliant and able man, a hard worker, and a serious student of Chinese classical learning. Coming to the throne as a boy, he achieved a reign of sixty years during which China returned to unification and prosperity. K'ang-hsi encouraged the traditional arts and crafts and established ateliers in the palace so that there would again be a national standard to follow.

In Chinese arts and crafts, we often talk about a Sung style, a Ming style, and so on as if the artistic trends followed the political changes or, more arbitrarily, the rise and fall of the dynasties. This was actually true to a large extent because of the important factor of imperial patronage. The period covering the disintegration of the Ming dynasty and the consolidation of power of the Ch'ing dynasty, which roughly extended over the last two-thirds of the seventeenth century, when imperial patronage was nonexistent, is known—particularly to scholars of Chinese ceramics—as the transition period. It was a period when, in order to survive, craftsmen tried to please many—the rich, the not-so-rich, and even the foreigners who had begun to buy Chinese products.

They had to cut costs and improve or modify their products to appeal to whoever had the money to pay, and at the same time they had to survive competition. Initiative took the place of the slavish following of court edicts. This period of transition was important in giving Chinese craftsmen the chance to do independent experimenting, and many technical improvements resulted.

The main innovations during this period were the phasing out of the standard Ming handwrought bronze wire and the adoption of copper wire manufactured through the process of drawplates. The reason was largely an economic one—cost had become an important consideration when there was no hope of imperial patronage. This innovation meant easier production of wires, less working time, and cheaper production costs.

There were other innovations, not necessarily all economic, but contributions to refinement—for instance, the discontinuation of the use of solder eliminated the chance of its melting, bubbling up, and discoloring the enamels; better control of firing created a smoother surface with fewer pits and bubbles in the enamels; the development of additional enamel colors greatly enhanced the naturalistic designs that could be made. Finally, a small change—small, yet important: a true pink of the so-called famille rose color was introduced from the West toward the end of K'ang-hsi's reign. It made unnecessary and obsolete the so-called Ming pink, a salami-like mixture of red and white particles used to induce an illusion of pink. The presence of this new pink is a sure sign that a piece is no earlier than the eighteenth century.

It is well to remind readers here that, although Ming pieces have bronze bodies, bronze wires, and salami-like mixtures of red and white enamels to give an illusion of pink, not every object with any or all of these features is necessarily Ming. In fact, it will be helpful for the reader to remember that the reverse of any well-established rule is not always true in the difficult field of identification and authentication.* These features were occasionally incorporated into cloisonné down to the present century, particularly when manufacturers consciously copied Ming wares, even including the reign mark under the foot.

The palace ateliers consolidated the innovations mentioned above, and they were adopted in turn by private producers all over the country. This was the start of a national trend or style. In his long sixty-year reign, K'ang-hsi's firm hand guided not only national affairs but also the arts and crafts of his time. A Ch'ing style came into being.

K'ang-hsi's efforts were further reinforced by his two successors. His son Yung-cheng (1723-1735) is pictured in fictionalized history as a cruel man, but he was actually a good administrator. His tastes ran slightly to the classical

---

*Many small items continued to be made with bronze body and bronze wires, such as snuff bottles, matchboxes, water pipes, and even cigarette lighter casings. (Has anybody seen a Ming cigarette lighter?) Sometimes the gilded wire was mistaken for bronze. Japanese items are still often made of bronze, with bronze wires.

52. K'ang-hsi era bowl with goldfish, Buddha's-hand citron, and realistic lotus and leaf motifs. Diameter 12 inches. *Dorothy Adler Routh Collection*

53. Boy with hobbyhorse and dog; K'ang-hsi era. Height 7 inches. *Dorothy Adler Routh Collection*

side, and there was a conspicuous return to copying the best that had been produced during the Sung and Ming periods, along with a love of archaism for archaism's sake. All these stylistic differences are clearly discernible in China's major craft, porcelain. Among discriminating collectors Yung-cheng wares rate deservedly high. However, in the case of cloisonné, a minor craft, it is not so easy to point out the differences between the two reigns. The pieces were often unmarked, and not enough identifiable pieces exist to draw any meaningful conclusions. The relatively small number surviving today are vases, incense burners, and pricket candlesticks, which were so standard in shape, form, and decoration that it is impossible to find any stylistic difference among them.

Yung-cheng's son, Ch'ien-lung (1736-1795), is universally considered as even more art-loving than his predecessors, although less discriminating. His tastes ranged from the classical to the ornate and even baroque; thus, according to art critics, he opened the door to decadence.

Ch'ien-lung was well liked as a ruler, an unusual achievement for a Manchu. The country was prosperous and the bitter anti-Manchu feeling had largely dissipated. He lived the life of a Chinese scholar-gentleman, collecting art and antiques, writing poetry, and practicing calligraphy. He was open-minded enough to have part of his palace built in the Western style, and he enjoyed the company of Westerners—among them, Castiglione and other Jesuits were his favorites. Not wanting to exceed the sixty-year rule of his illustrious grandfather, K'ang-hsi, he retired after fifty-nine years and let his son ascend the dragon throne.

What is important to us in discussing Chinese cloisonné is that there is definitely a Ch'ien-lung style. For one thing, many of the pieces produced during his reign were marked accordingly. For another, more pieces are in existence, and so a detailed study can be made and a comparison with products of the other periods is possible. Third, the emperor seemed to be actively interested in this craft and probably provided guidelines for the craftsmen to follow. Besides the standard temple pieces (some measured six feet in height) that the emperor by tradition distributed as gifts to the various Lama temples,* a great variety of shapes and forms was made. Human figures and animal shapes were particularly popular. The endless list includes such unusual items as wine pots in the shape of ducks, candlesticks in the shape of cranes, copies of archaic bronze vessels, and even birdcages, doghouses, and ice chests. All were heavily gilded and overpowering to the viewer.

The basic attraction of Ch'ien-lung cloisonné is its grandeur, which is pronounced and emphasized. The pieces were characterized by massiveness. Even in small items, the feeling of massiveness still prevails. The wires were heavy and the enamels were thickly applied in solid brilliant colors, slightly more opaque in comparison to those on Ming specimens but perhaps more effective.

*A Buddhist sect favored by the Manchu rulers.

54. Pair of quaillike birds with removable backs, made in the style of Ch'ien-lung. Height 7 inches. *Dorothy Adler Routh Collection*

55. Boy on water buffalo; style of Ch'ien-lung. Length 4½ inches. *Dorothy Adler Routh Collection*

56. Stylized bird with removable back, in the Ch'ien-lung style. Length 4½ inches. *Dorothy Adler Routh Collection*

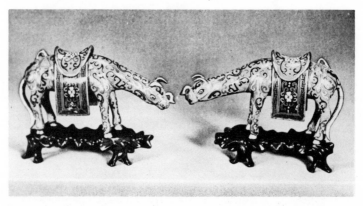

57. Pair of unicorn-type beasts, in the style, of Ch'ien-lung. Length 7 inches. *Dorothy Adler Routh Collection*

58. Willow pattern plate in blue and white cloisonné. Diameter 12 inches. Probably early nineteenth century. *Dorothy Adler Routh Collection*

The art of Chinese cloisonné reached its summit during the reign of Ch'ien-lung. After that, there could be only decline. In substituting ornateness for art, the emperor may indeed have sown the seeds of decadence—for not only in cloisonné, but in the great ceramic industry as well, decadence set in during the long and prosperous reign of Ch'ien-lung.

59. Water dropper with bronze body decorated with polychrome enamels on turquoise ground; Ch'ien-lung period. Even in small objects, the feeling of massiveness prevails. Diameter approx. 3 inches. *Keller & Scott, Carmel, California*

6

The Age of Export—
Late Nineteenth Century
to the Present

AFTER THE CH'IEN-LUNG PERIOD, a time of false prosperity in which the emperor spent much but the country did not produce enough to match the lavish court expense, the Ch'ing dynasty went downhill, and with it the arts and crafts of China.

Politically, there was the long-lasting anti-Manchu T'ai-ping Rebellion, which lay waste a large part of China; this was followed by small uprisings from about 1880 on. In foreign relations the Manchu government was also inept, unable to cope with the increasing contacts with other nations. There were the Opium War of 1840 and the Sino-Japanese War in 1894. And in 1900 the ignorant and headstrong Empress Dowager, in a foolhardy anti-West campaign, precipitated the crisis of the Boxer Rebellion. Foreign troops repeatedly marched on Peking, burned the palaces, and looted their treasures.

Finally, in 1912, an almost bloodless revolution overthrew the Ch'ing dynasty, but the newly formed republic was so conciliatory that the dethroned boy emperor was permitted to live in the palace on a government pension and to keep the art treasures. A great deal of stealing was done by the suddenly impoverished royal relatives and by avaricious eunuchs and servants. Priceless treasures assembled and personally authenticated by the Emperors K'ang-hsi, Yung-cheng, and Ch'ien-lung were sold all over Peking for a song—it was a great age for foreign collectors and art dealers. These treasures, plus those looted by the foreign troops, can now be seen in great museums all over the world.

60. Heavy flat bowl with rust red enamel and intricate wire design inside and outside. Diameter 10 inches.

61. Reverse of the bowl in Ill. 60. It is light blue under the foot, with the reign mark in pink enamel: "Made in the Ch'ien-lung Period." Possibly of the period.

62. Heavy flat bowl in polychrome enamels, including a fine pink. Diameter 8 inches.

63. Reverse of the bowl in Ill. 62. The mark says: "Made in the Great Ming Period"; but the piece is definitely not of the period.

64. Double gourd-shaped snuff bottle with bronze ribbons and polychrome enamels on turquoise ground. Height approx. 5 inches. *Keller & Scott, Carmel, California*

65. Elegant bottle-shaped vase with close lotus scroll decor. Height approx. 6 inches. *Keller & Scott, Carmel, California*

66. Cast maker's mark on the base of Ill. 65.

67. Heavy bronze stirrup with simple cloisonné decoration. This was not made for export. However, the co-operative Chinese exporters did make cheap stirrup-shaped ashtray sets (usually four in progressively diminished sizes that could be stacked inside the stirrup). Many were made in stamped relief and thinly coated with enamels.

68. Fine box with precocious Chinese baby boy among flowers. *Mr. & Mrs. Ray Wentworth Collection*

69. Cribbage board. *Keller & Scott, Carmel, California*

70. In old China, only scholars and tailors wore spectacles—the former because they could afford them, the latter from necessity. (Remember, the lenses were usually made of natural crystal of the purest and finest quality.) Even though fourteenth-century connoisseurs denounced cloisonné as fit only for the lady's boudoir, tastes must have changed during the Ch'ing dynasty. No scholar, however, need be ashamed of carrying a spectacle case like this one. On the front are lotus flowers and waterweeds matching the best in painting of the literati school. The enamel colors are of the utmost softness and delicacy, with a barely visible tint of pink on the flowers.

71. The reverse of the spectacle case in Ill. 70. The stalk of bamboo, the plant of strength and character, is a medium blue green. The background is black, now softly matte in finish. Both the body and wires are made of bronze, so that no vulgar copperish red would offend the learned user. Ca. 1850.

70.   71.

72. Cigarette box. To heighten their enjoyment, addicts of Chinese opera chewed tidbits, drank tea, and smoked profusely during a performance. This box was made for such an opera fan. On the cover are the two contesting generals: the red face (the good guy) and the white face (the bad guy). Needless to say, the red face always prevails. The side panels show the paraphernalia used in Chinese opera.

73. Front panel of the cigarette box in Ill. 72, with an actor's boots, hat, and mask.

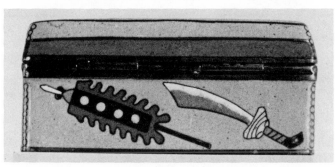

74. Rear panel of the cigarette box in Ill. 72, with a banner and sword.

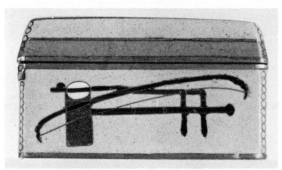

75. One end panel of the same cigarette box shows the Chinese violin that accompanies the singing.

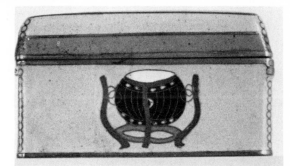

76. On the other end panel of the cigarette box is the drum.

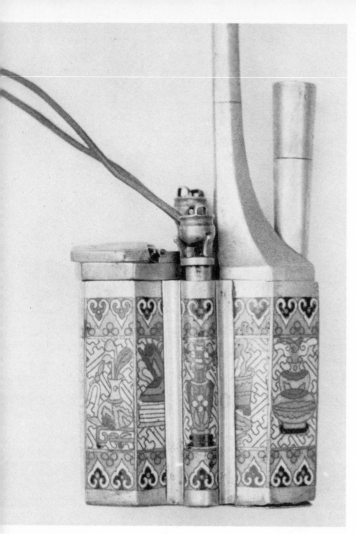

77. Not all opera fans liked "foreign smoke" or cigarettes. The real connoisseurs, in particular, preferred the Chinese water-cooled pipes that many Americans mistakenly call opium pipes. But it was a nuisance to carry a pipe to the theatre—it was quite heavy and the water was likely to spill and stain the owner's silk gown. Therefore there were always "smoke-sellers," just as we have hot-dog vendors at a baseball game. For a few coppers, the operagoer could secure the service of a smoke-seller who would fill the pipe, light it up, and keep it burning for the customer. But for the pipe to reach the smoker in a crowded theatre, the stem had to be long—sometimes over two feet. Shown here is a white bronze water pipe with the hundred antiques on *wan* or T ground. *Keller & Scott, Carmel, California*

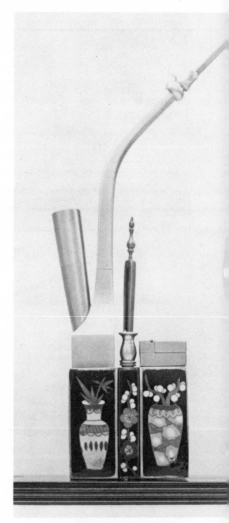

78. Another water pipe, which has the hundred antiques decor on a plain background.

Plate 1. Incense perfumer, cloisonné enamel, Ching-t'ai ware (1450-1457), Ming dynasty. *Collection of the National Palace Museum, Taipei, Taiwan, Republic of China*

Plate 2. Plate with dragon decoration, cloisonné enamel, Wan-li ware (1573-1620), Ming dynasty. *Collection of the National Palace Museum, Taipei, Taiwan, Republic of China*

Plate 3. Cloisonné jar with swing handle and "T'ao-t'ieh" decor, Ch'ien-lung ware (1736-1795), Ch'ing dynasty. *Collection of the National Palace Museum, Taipei, Taiwan, Republic of China*

Plate 4. Cloisonné *tsun*, wine vessel, on the back of a phoenix, Ch'ing dynasty. *Collection of the National Palace Museum, Taipei, Taiwan, Republic of China*

Plate 5. Chinese cloisonné vase; so-called openwork technique. Height 9¾ inches. *Walter Chandoha Collection*

Plate 6. Chinese cloisonné vase. Height 24½ inches, Ch'ing dynasty. *Walter Chandoha Collection*

Plate 7. Japanese cloisonné with traditional designs.

Plate 8. The jardiniere and the pedestal at left are Japanese cloisonné. On the tables (*left to right*): Chinese cloisonné potiche, Japanese cloisonné vase, Chinese cloisonné bulb bowl, Japanese cloisonné vase, Chinese cloisonné tea jar, Japanese and Chinese cloisonné vases. On the wall are Chinese painted enamel and cloisonné trays. *Bottom row*: Chinese cloisonné millefleur vase, covered melon dish and plate in translucent enamel, Japanese cloisonné screen, Chinese painted enamel dish, Japanese cloisonné tea jar, and Chinese cloisonné gourd vase.

Plate 9. Japanese cloisonné enamel; diameter 12 inches. *Walter Chandoha Collection*

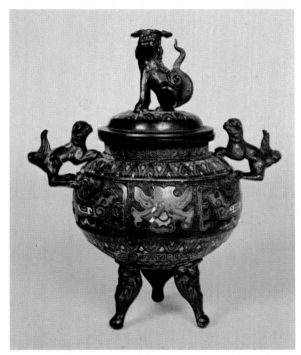

Plate 10. Japanese champlevé incense burner. Height 10½ inches. *Walter Chandoha Collection*

Plate 11. Japanese vases with naturalistic designs.

Plate 12. Modern Japanese translucent-type cloisonné (mostly of the pigeon blood variety).

Plate 13. Modern Japanese cloisonné vases using silver foil as background. Note, in the bottom row, the brilliance created by combining translucent enamels of pastel colors and a silver background.

Plate 14. At far left is a Japanese tea jar. Second from left is the $10 Japanese vase of mistaken identity described in Chapter 7. The third piece is a Chinese vase of millefleur type, height 13 inches. The brush holder (*far right*) is Japanese cloisonné made on a pottery base.

Plate 15. Chinese painted enamels.

Plate 16. Various articles of Chinese translucent enamel work.

Plate 17. Damaged cloisonné vase pictured in the step-by-step repair process shown in Chapter 10.

Plate 18. The damaged vase in Plate 17 is shown here after restoration, along with a restored gourd-shaped vase and stem cups.

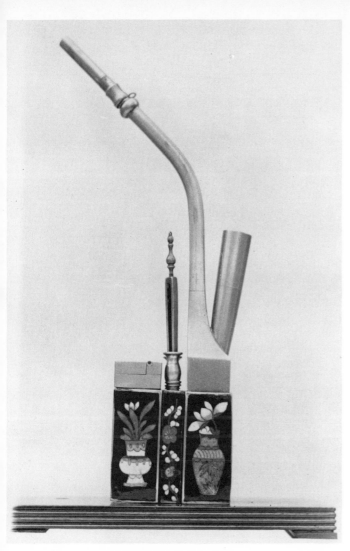

79. Reverse side of the water pipe in Ill. 78.

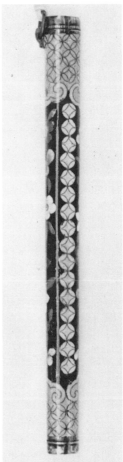

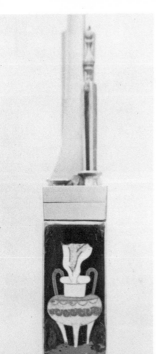

< 80. End view of the same water pipe in Ill. 78. (Both ends are the same.)

81. A survival kit? This tube contains a pair of ivory chopsticks and a small knife. When a man of means or prudence travels, he carries his own chopsticks.

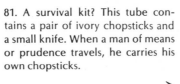

>

82. The brilliant colors of the cloisonné containers complement the beauty of the jade trees.

83. Heavy-duty tray with naturalistic floral decorations against a rust red background. Length 8 inches; width 6 inches.

As the Ch'ing dynasty went through crisis after crisis, the disappearance of —or a substantial decrease in—imperial patronage forced the various crafts to look elsewhere once more for financial support. There were always the landed gentry and the scholar-gentleman class, who also served as well-paid government officials. These men of taste and tradition continued to demand high quality and good workmanship.

At the same time, the West began to be fascinated by oriental products. The fad for chinoiserie ran strong and long. First the Dutch, then the French and English, and finally American merchants set up purchasing headquarters (notably, the various East India companies) in Canton and other coastal ports. These middlemen did not want quality. They wanted cheap goods and quick delivery, and they taught the native craftsmen how to cut corners—to lower costs and decrease weight so that shipping would not be as expensive. The result was that a tremendous quantity of shoddy merchandise was produced that makes up a large part of the oriental collectibles on the market today.

For the most part, cloisonné items exported during this era were mass-produced utilitarian articles such as ashtrays, napkin rings, salt and pepper sets, vases, and tea jars—of all shapes and forms. The metal bodies were very light, the enamels very thin and often badly pitted. To cover up the defects, colored wax was rubbed in the pits, which of course reappeared when the wax was gone. A slight fall, and one of these objects is badly dented, the enamels are splintered and loosened, and the wires broken. The smaller items were sold to foreign importers by the pound; the larger vases, by the inch. But even these cheap items, studiously ignored by connoisseurs, still represent a considerable amount of trained workmanship. And there is the matter of the talent of the individual workman: there is always the man who can consistently make more tasteful, more artistic products than hundreds of his less-talented fellows. Then, too, there was the stubborn pride (three generations in the business) of a maker who would rather starve than cheapen his product and lower his standards. The smart collector is one who constantly searches for and can spot the highest in artistic quality.

84. Box with design of two dragons contesting a flaming pearl in a cloud pattern over sea waves, with the so-called Rock of Ages in the center. Extremely fine wirework and very heavy. Ground is dark green. Dimensions 7 by 5 by 3 inches.

85. Tea jar with floral design on bright green ground in cloud diaper pattern. Height 8 inches; diameter 6 inches.

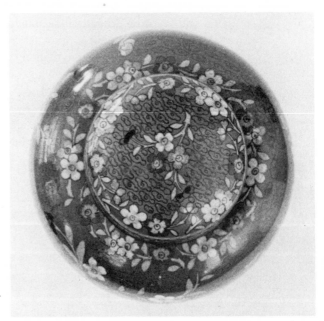

86. Top view of the jar in Ill. 85.

87. Large potiche with floral design. Many of these well-made cloisonné items were turned into lamps during the 1920s. Because of the protection provided by the often heavy bases and canopylike shades, they have suffered little or no damage and are always found in surprisingly good condition. Height 8½ inches. *Pinney Collection*

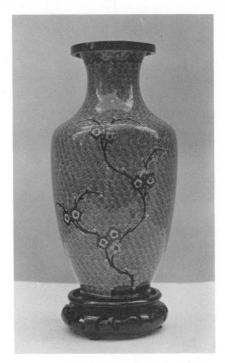

88. Very heavy vase with prunus design and scroll diaper pattern. Background is a lovely robin's-egg blue. Height 9 inches.

89. Vase with wave or fish-scale design on black ground—simplicity gives it a serene dignity. Height 7 inches.

90. Tray with continuous scrolls in rows. Diameter 7 inches.

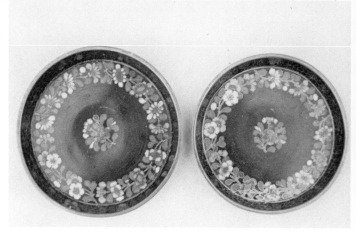

92. Exceptionally fine work on set of graduated trays that have a floral pattern against a black ground at the bottom. Sides are perpendicular and have minute designs on the top edge. Diameters 3½ and 4 inches.

91. Heavy and well-made vase with mille-fleur pattern in various shades of yellow and green to golden brown translucent enamel. Height 11 inches.

93. Potiche with floral design on a black ground with *wan* or T diaper pattern. Height 9 inches; diameter 7 inches.

94. Miniature potiche with stylized prunus flowers on black ground; scroll diaper pattern. Height 3 inches.

95. Vase with formal lotus and buds on white background; cloud diaper pattern. Height 6 inches.

96. Vase with formal peony and leaves in polychrome enamels on off-white ground. Height 6 inches.

98. Vase with formalized millefleur design in polychrome enamels, bright yellows and greens predominating. Height 13 inches.

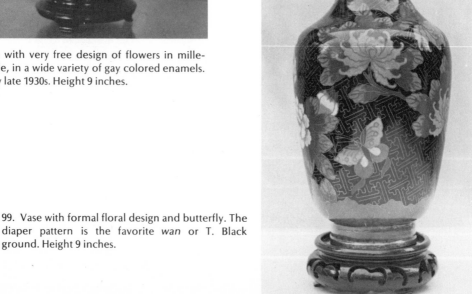

97. Vase with very free design of flowers in millefleur style, in a wide variety of gay colored enamels. Probably late 1930s. Height 9 inches.

99. Vase with formal floral design and butterfly. The diaper pattern is the favorite *wan* or T. Black ground. Height 9 inches.

100. Vase of exquisite floral design with triangular diaper pattern on black ground. Height 13 inches.

101. Candlestick (or lamp base) with floral design on black ground. Diaper pattern is *wan* or T. Height 13 inches.

102. Vase with dragon chasing pearl in a cloud scroll diaper pattern; sky-blue background. Height 13 inches.

104. Tray with the longevity character in the center of scroll diaper pattern. Diameter 7 inches.

103. Vase with a different dragon design. Stiff leaves and ling-chi (sacred mushroom) motif appear on the neck. Height 9 inches.

106. Domed cigarette box with fish scale or wave and *wan* diaper pattern on a black ground. Height 3 inches.

105. White peony design with turquoise ground and cloud diaper pattern. Height 9 inches.

107. Domed cigarette box with floral scroll and wave diaper pattern on black ground. Height 3 inches.

108. Domed cigarette box showing an unusually free design of a foreign sailor fishing in the sea (a caricature?). Ca. 1930. Height 3 inches.

109. Reverse side of the box in Ill. 108.

111. Squat vase with peony design, *wan* or T diaper pattern, and a black ground. Height 7 inches; diameter 6 inches.

110. Top of the cigarette box shown in Ill. 108.

112. Small incense burner in lotus scroll pattern on white ground has gilded copper legs and monster-mask ring handles.

113. Small potiche with white floral design on black ground. Diaper pattern is the popular *wan* or T.

114. Double gourds on vines, a favorite Chinese subject, decorate this vase. Height 7 inches.

115. White prunus on a true apple-green ground. No diaper pattern breaks the pleasing smoothness of the vase surface. Height 9 inches.

116. Flat covered bowl with wave diaper pattern in deep turquoise green. Diameter 6 inches.

117. Rice bowl without foot rim is decorated with flowers on a green ground and cloud diaper pattern. Diameter 4¼ inches.

118. Bottom of the bowl in Ill. 117 showing lotus petal design. "China" is embedded in the enamels with wire.

119. Rice bowl in bright yellows, greens, and pinks. Diameter 4½ inches.

120. Larger bowl with lotus flowers against a deep red ground and cloud diaper pattern. Diameter 5 inches.

121. Set of four wine cups. Diameter 1¼ inches.

122. Pair of small jars with black ground; *wan* and wave diaper pattern. Diameter 2 inches.

123. Salt and pepper set—scroll wire-work with black enamel.

124. Set of three items with the same type of dragons on each; black enamel on a mustard yellow ground with cloud diaper pattern.

125. "Openwork" tray with stylized Indian lotus, leaves, and scrolls. Diameter 3½ inches.

126. This casket-style cigarette box, with bird and prunus design on an apple green background, is an export item of better than average quality.

127. Rectangular covered box with a floral design in polychrome enamels on a black ground; 6 by 4½ by 1½ inches. *Walter Chandoha Collection*

128. Casket-type hinged box with dragon design on a black ground; 6½ by 2½ by 2½ inches. *Walter Chandoha Collection*

129. Seal box with floral design on red ground; 4½ by 2 by 2 inches (approx.). *Walter Chandoha Collection*

130. Rectangular box with turquoise floral design on white ground; 7½ by 3½ by 1¼ inches (approx.). *Walter Chandoha Collection*

131. Tea jar with floral design on a green ground. Height 7 inches. *Walter Chandoha Collection*

132. Potiche with floral design on rust red ground. Height 9 inches. *Walter Chandoha Collection*

133. Potiche with design of double gourds on green ground. Height 7½ inches. *Walter Chandoha Collection*

134. Export type of ashtray with two bare curved bronze pieces for resting lighted cigarettes. Diameter 4½ inches.

135. Napkin ring made exclusively for export. (The Chinese never use napkin rings.) This type of thing, sold to foreign importers by the pound, often represents the poorest workmanship.

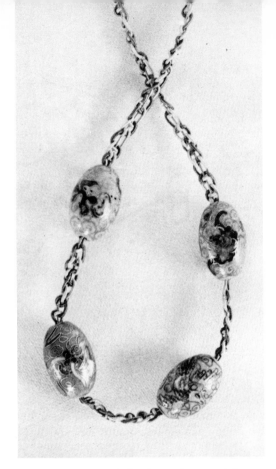

138. Four cloisonné beads, each one different. Starting from the point where the chain crosses and going clockwise: a bat, a phoenix, a dragon, and a peach. Designs are in polychrome enamels on robin's-egg blue ground.

136. Two designs of matchbox holders. They were typical export items from 1920 on.

137. Earrings decorated with flowers in colored enamels on a white ground. Ca. 1920.

This, of course, is only a thumbnail summary of five centuries of Chinese cloisonné production—a minor art or craft at first described as unfit for the scholar-gentlemen's chaste taste, but one that gradually gained recognition and even imperial patronage during the K'ang-hsi and Ch'ien-lung reigns. The biggest change in the manufacturing process seems to have occurred between the Ming and Ch'ing dynasties—roughly, during the last two-thirds of the seventeenth century—and the differences between the cloisonnés of the two dynasties are easily perceptible. The following summary can be used as an aid in identification:

1

MING: Bronze wires. According to Harry Garner, the wires on early specimens often show longitudinal splits because of improper annealing. Bodies of early wares are often made of cast bronze.

CH'ING: Copper wires made through the use of drawplates or dies. Bodies hammered from copper sheets.

2

MING: Traces of solder boiled up to the surface.

CH'ING: Solder eliminated in favor of a temporary adhesive that burned away during firing.

3

MING: Enamels were limited to dark blackish green, white, turquoise blue and (later) turquoise green, yellow, red, and cobalt blue (this was a beautiful purple blue when Mohammedan blue was available, and later grayish when native cobalt was first used). More pits and more air bubbles because the enamel paste was less well prepared and the packing and firing methods were cruder.*

CH'ING: The colors were more extensive, notably a true pink and brighter greens and yellows of many shades. Fewer air bubbles apparent.

4

MING: Motifs were limited to highly stylized lotus scrolls, stiff leaves, dragons and other mythical creatures, and wave patterns. Some naturalistic themes.

CH'ING: Besides the above-named traditional motifs, there were more naturalistic ones, as well as a profusion of *t'ao-t'ieh* masks and *kuei* dragons. These pseudoarchaic bronze motifs were particularly popular during the Ch'ien-lung period.

*Another explanation for the large number of holes and bubbles in the Ming cloisonné is that they were caused by the zinc in the bronze (strictly speaking, brass) bodies and wires. Zinc tends to vaporize during firing, causing air bubbles and holes in the enamels. The substitution of copper for bronze (brass) helped eliminate some of these imperfections.

5
MING: Traditional shapes and forms.
CH'ING: The addition of human and animal figures.

In recent years the production of cloisonné has been resumed on a quite large scale. From China come export articles of fine quality and workmanship, with deservedly high prices. The designs and decorations are traditional as well as naturalistic and hardly distinguishable from those made during the early 1900s. An occasional item with a revolutionary theme will appear on the market, perhaps brought out by travelers. Such pieces are apparently made for home consumption. Taiwan also makes small cloisonné items, although these are not often seen on the market.

139. Bracelet with floral design in shades of translucent browns and opaque black and white enamels. Submerged cloisonné wires are visible under the enamel. Recent import from Taiwan.

140A. Pair of vases recently made and imported from Peking. These are better quality, with fewer pits and brighter-colored enamels, than those made before World War II. The design is very traditional. A pair like these retails in the United States for about $200. *Courtesy of Scanlan Imports—The Prune Yard, Campbell, California*

140B. Another vase of recent import from mainland China. The workmanship is impeccable. Colors are bright green, shocking pink, and bright lavender. Note the rolled lip of both this vase and the pair in 140A. ➤

Japanese
Cloisonné –
The Early Period

Browsing in a small antique shop, we found a Japanese cloisonné vase about twelve inches high with exquisite designs of birds and cherry blossoms on a sky-blue background. The price astonished us. Ten dollars! It was worth over $100. (See Color Plate 14.)

We took it to the counter and paid the ten dollars.

The proprietor, who looked like and had the bearing of a retired naval officer, took our money and made out the receipt: "Porcelain vase—$10, tax 50¢." Then he wrote "Paid in full" with a flourish of fine antique script and gave the receipt to us.

"It is a *cloisonné* vase, though," one of us murmured with polite embarrassment.

"Oh, is it?" He put on his glasses and took a close look. "Sure enough. It's

141. Vase sold to the authors for ten dollars as porcelain. It has a dazzling bright blue background. The pheasants are in naturalistic colors—bright yellows and oranges. The cherry blossoms are very realistic in pink and white. Height 11 inches; diameter at mouth 4 inches.

a fine piece of Japanese cloisonné. I bought it just yesterday and really didn't have time to look at it closely. A cloisonné vase like this should be worth—"

"We know. Tell us, how much do you really want for it?"

"Ten dollars."

"But we don't want you to cheat yourself."

"Look—see the sign over there? ALL SALES FINAL. I put the sign there, and I'd better stick to it."

People do make mistakes about modern Japanese cloisonné because it is not only exquisitely made, with the wires hardly visible, but it is less familiar to Westerners than Chinese pieces. In fact, many beginning collectors look bemused when confronted with the term "Japanese cloisonné." A lady once asked us in a puzzled tone, "Isn't all oriental cloisonné made by the Chinese?"

The answer is that around 75 percent of the cloisonné items on the market today were made in China. Since about 1900, Chinese exporters have engaged in the lucrative export of cheap, lightweight, and hastily made cloisonné articles, such as ashtrays, napkin rings, salt and pepper sets, and cigarette boxes. Most of the tedious work, such as packing the cells with enamel paste, was done by women and children, on a production line, each doing a small part without needing to possess the skill or the experience gained by apprenticeship training. As a result, the quality of these items was shoddy; they were rough and the enamels were badly pitted. To correct this last defect, a generous amount of wax was rubbed in as a cover-up.

Japanese makers, on the other hand, did not engage in the mass export of cloisonné. Their products were always made with meticulous care by trained and competent craftsmen. Every wire was put in carefully according to the design. One never detects the slapdash workmanship that was done by men engaged in mass production.

There are those who prefer the robustness and even the slightly unfinished quality of Chinese cloisonné to the exquisite and careful workmanship of the Japanese. They often criticize the Japanese works as being effeminate. This is certainly unjustified. We feel both types have their merits. They are just different—different in many ways.

Chinese cloisonné—the well-made, nonexport type—tends to overpower the senses with its magnificence, its flamboyance, its stylized decorative motifs, its sheer massive form and weight (features inherited from the archaic Chinese bronze), and the brilliant contrast of bright colors and heavy gilding. Chinese cloisonné instantly and constantly commands attention; even a large room can accommodate no more than one large piece or a pair (as the Chinese prefer). In an aesthetic sense, however, Japanese cloisonné appeals with a very different kind of attraction. One can have a roomful of Japanese items without being overwhelmed by their presence.

To achieve their particular result, the Japanese craftsmen made many innovations in the art during the late nineteenth century. To attain delicacy of design, minimize the harsh separation of the cloisons, and produce specimens as naturalistic as a brush painting, they used wires as fine as—often finer than —hair and worked them into intricate patterns. Wires of different metals or alloys were sometimes used in a single piece—silver for the flowers, copper and bronze for the leaves.

For all these reasons, art historians seem to feel that Japanese cloisonné may have had a different origin from the Chinese. Perhaps the Japanese learned the art directly from the Middle Eastern countries, since in the fifteenth and sixteenth centuries commerce by the open sea increased rapidly and the direct exchange of cultural and artistic traditions was greatly facilitated.

Some scholars believe that, during the early part of the seventeenth century, the Japanese mastered the technique of cloisonné-making. In the city museum of Osaka, Japan, is an apparently very old, small crucifix. Since the Tokugawa Shogunate had issued an edict outlawing the Christian religion in 1614, so the reasoning goes, the crucifix must have been made before the order was promulgated. However, the evidence is perhaps as tenuous at best as the controversial mirror in the Sho-so-in (see footnote page 33). One swallow does not make a summer. Unless an art form has taken root sufficiently to occupy the creative efforts of at least a small part of the citizenry, there is no use speculating on its date of inception. Furthermore, the Christian religion did not disappear during the persecution but went underground; and the Japanese Christians around Nagasaki became known as the Hiding Christians. The above-mentioned crucifix could very well have been made by the Hiding Christians at a much later date. Or the crucifix could have been brought in by European traders or missionaries before 1614. Europeans at that time were quite advanced in the art of enameling.

Another school of art historians theorizes that, like certain other crafts and skills, Japan also learned cloisonné-making from China. This theory is supported by the fact that the earliest full-fledged Japanese cloisonné work in the form of vases, jars, wine pots, cups, and other items indispensable to the amenities of gracious oriental living shows only slight differences from the Chinese work when the important elements of design, motif, quality of the enamels, and workmanship are carefully analyzed. These early pieces, clumsy in shape and form, timidly repetitive in motif and design, show a self-consciousness and conformity typical of the early apprenticeship stage of a newly introduced art. It is apparent that Japanese cloisonné at this time, unlike the other China-originated arts such as painting, lacquer, and porcelain, which the Japanese had not only mastered but in a sense Japanized to suit their national temperament, was still in the experimental stage.

As we have already shown, the art of cloisonné-making was a rather late development in the Orient. In China this new art form was probably brought in by the Mongols, who established the short-lived Yüan dynasty (1277-1368), which the Ming dynasty (1368-1644) overthrew. The Mongols were great conquerors. Many divergent cultures were brought together by the process of military expansion. Marco Polo came to China and served the Yüan court and, returning home, took Chinese cuisine, pizza, ravioli, and spaghetti (but not chop suey) to the Western world. Conversely, many arts and crafts were introduced to China, among them the art of cloisonné, then practiced by the Persians and the Arabians, many of whom were transported to China by the conquerors. By the early Ming dynasty, during the reign of the Emperor Hsüan-te (1426-1435), Chinese craftsmen had already mastered the technique and were producing magnificent specimens in this imported art form.

If the Japanese did learn the art from the Chinese, which is the more tenable assumption, it would not have taken them long, with their native adaptability, to master it. But we can be sure Japan did not adopt this new art form until much later. Because of the unsuccessful attempts by the Mongols to conquer Japan, she had raised her guard and cut off nearly all intercourse with the mainland. The ascendency of the Ming dynasty brought with it a return to

142. This is probably the oldest type of large Japanese cloisonné specimen available today. The design consists entirely of a brocade pattern, although there are two distinct panels, one in front and one in the back. The shape is ungainly, like that of most early Japanese cloisonné items. This piece is about two feet tall; the body is lightweight, being made of thin copper sheeting. Ca. 1830. *From private collection of Philip Wood*

143. Design on the reverse side of the vessel shown in Ill. 142.

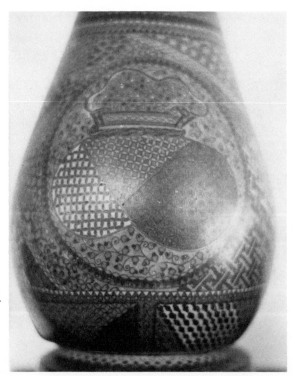

144. Detail of the panel illustrated in Ill. 143.

the traditional peace-loving Confucian way of life and a normal relationship between the Asiatic countries. This relationship was shattered again during the late Ming period by the ambitious attempt of the Japanese military to invade Korea and China. Japanese campaigns laid waste Korea, which had always served as a bridge for cultural inflow from the mainland; the bridge then acted more often as a barrier than a conduit.

Those who continued to make the attempt to reach China were mostly painters, scholars, and Zen monks, whose cultured tastes would naturally be offended by such gaudy displays as cloisonné, which besides carried the double onus of not being native Chinese but barbarian and therefore inferior. The scholars and artists who made the trip by sea were interested only in learning the Sung and Ming method of landscape painting. The Zen monks admired simplicity in life; it would not be reasonable to expect that these monks, who had brought back the rustic teabowls of Fukien as treasures, would carry home ornate cloisonné pieces on their return trip. Rather, it may have been the Korean porcelain makers, brought back by Hideyoshi's expeditionary forces (1592-1593), who happened to know something of the craft of making cloisonné. Indeed, it might even have been the Japanese pirates who repeatedly raided the Chinese coast. Pirates are not noted for their discriminating taste. The same thing could perhaps be said of the daimyos (feudal lords) and the rich merchants of Japan—the Tokugawa period was noted for its love of ornate decorative articles.

For several hundred years before the emperor was returned to power in 1868, Japan was a feudal state ruled, under the overall dictatorship of the Shogun, by many daimyos or feudal lords who not only owned the land but also the people and the craftsmen living on it. Each jealously guarded the secrets of whatever crafts thrived in his domain—pottery, porcelain, silk, or brocade manufacture. Divulging the manufacturing secrets of these industries was often punishable by death.* For this reason, few reliable records exist, particularly in the case of such a relatively minor craft as cloisonné. The information we have found in Japanese sources seems inadequate or conflicting. Fortunately, dating is not a crucial matter in Japanese cloisonné, since few of the objects on the market are over 100 years old. Collectors need not be too concerned about the problem.†

The genius of the Japanese craftsmen does not depend upon their inventiveness, but upon their ability to adapt imported processes and mediums and then work hard to surpass the achievements of the originating country, and finally, to endow the product with a feeling and appearance that are uniquely Japanese. Lacquering, for instance (because lacquer is an important branch of

---

*It is interesting to note that during the fifteenth century, Murano glassworkers also risked severe punishment if they left Venice and gave away their trade secrets.
†The theory that the Japanese had a golden age of cloisonné art that was forgotten and then revived during the early nineteenth century has been proven groundless.

oriental crafts or even art), Japan learned from China. Yet the Japanese worked at it, particularly during their periods of isolation from the mainland, until they surpassed all other oriental lacquer-producing countries in smooth workmanship, in the sophisticated use of gold in various shades, and in naturalistic designs. Even the Ming Chinese were so impressed that they sent craftsmen to learn the Japanese methods. The Japanese were justly proud—they had bettered their teachers.

However, this overemphasis on lacquer, a versatile craft that still is used for many decorative and utilitarian Japanese articles today, had profound influence on other arts and crafts. Mastery of it was achieved at the expense of other crafts. Many art historians believe it was the infatuation with lacquer that delayed the production of porcelain in Japan until the seventeenth century. It is therefore only reasonable to conclude that such a novelty as cloisonné, perhaps frowned upon by the tea masters (who occupied practically the same position as the scholars or the literati in China), the arbiters of taste in those days, who preferred the simple and rustic, could attract little favorable attention when it was first made in Japan. Nor has it ever been able to compete with lacquer, pottery, and porcelain.

Cloisonné probably had a slow and laborious beginning. There was, to start with, the problem of making enamels. The Romans, the Arabians, the French, and the Chinese, who had made glass early and knew how to color it expertly, had only to perfect the fusible glass paste. But Japan was not a glass-producing country, and suitable material was not easily available for enamel work (although the method of making glass was known there as early as the seventh or eighth century through her contact with her neighbors on the continent), and so some experimenting with the glass paste technique had to be done before cloisonné could be successfully produced. It was not, however, a great hurdle to go from the colored glazes and overglaze enamels used in the decoration of pottery to the making of cloisonné enamels. Perhaps those intended for pottery decoration were first drafted to serve the purpose of the new craft of cloisonné. Indeed, the early Japanese enamel colors were rather drab, and they did not succeed in making a good turquoise blue until the late nineteenth century.

The Japanese called cloisonné *shippo*, the term used to designate seven precious metals and stones: gold, silver, green glass (or green-colored semiprecious stones), crystal, pearl, agate, and coral. The term can refer to both the inlaid "seven precious things" (*shippo kan*) and the fused "seven precious things" (*shippo nagashi*)—meaning cloisonné. The earliest specimens, in fact, all show approximately the same palette—notably: yellow, red, blue, and white, on a dark green background. Other colors were added slowly—for instance, a gold-sprinkled translucent brown. This brown, slightly somber to the modern eye, is perhaps a carry-over from lacquer, which in Japan has always been the leading art form.

The earliest Japanese cloisonné products are not too different from the

Chinese. It is sometimes difficult, if not impossible, to distinguish the one from the other because of their overall complicated designs and motifs. This similarity resulted from the fact that the early cloisonné workers always felt the need for close wirework to anchor the enamels and prevent them from cracking. However, there are differences: the Chinese always used the Indian lotus motif, which swerves gracefully and fills the spaces quite adequately without crowding; on the other hand, the Japanese diaper patterns consisting of floral and leaf designs (the favorite being a type of aquatic weed) appear to be brocadelike and geometrical. The Chinese often placed their principal motif in two or four panels, if panels were used at all, one on each side of the vase, but the Japanese liked to subdivide the surface into several panels—round, square, and/or fan-shaped. At first the Chinese background was always bright turquoise and the Japanese a dark green.

As far as the decorative subjects were concerned, they came mostly from the same Chinese mythological sources. The "three friends of the cold weather" (the pine, the bamboo, and the prunus), the phoenix (Japanese *hoo*), and the dragon are favorite motifs of both countries. The Chinese consider the dragon

145. Bowl decorated with good luck and longevity characters along with typical Japanese designs, although the mark on the base says "Great Ming." Diameter approx. 8 inches. Ca. 1870. *Dr. & Mrs. Marvin Hockabout Collection*

146. Base of the bowl in Ill. 145. Note the "Great Ming" mark.

a symbol of great majestic importance, with the five-claw type reserved for the imperial family and the four-claw for lesser nobility and high officials. The Japanese make no such distinction with the dragon. Theirs show three sharp claws and are more sinuous. Another difference is that the Japanese follow the custom of using *mon* (emblems, such as the formal round chrysanthemum and the paulownia flower) for decoration. These symbols on an article always indicate Japanese origin.

Also helpful in identification is the shape or form of an article. Roughly, the craftsmen in each country followed the shapes and forms already created by their potters and also their bronze workers. Their ceramic industries had already been in existence for hundreds of years and had developed favorite shapes and forms, which the cloisonné craftsmen could readily appropriate. It should be mentioned, however, that attempts must have been made by the earliest Japanese craftsmen to create their own shapes and forms, for they produced the ugliest and most ungainly things ever made in the Orient. These shapes and forms, to their credit, the cloisonné makers soon dropped.

Pre-1800 specimens of Japanese cloisonné vessels are extremely rare and usually of doubtful attribution. Therefore, writers on the subject rightly start with the early 1800s, when Japanese craftsmen began not only to produce in quantity, but also to develop a distinct style of their own.

147. Knife and its cloisonné sheath. The design is very simple, the enamels quite primitive. It is probably early Japanese work, although the possibility of Mideastern or Chinese origin cannot be ruled out. *Keller & Scott, Carmel, California*

8

Japanese
Cloisonné –
The Peak and the Decline

REPEATED STERN EDICTS OF THE TOKUGAWA REGIME called for austerity and the restoration of the ways of the warriors, but the fun-loving, affluent and decoration-conscious citizens persisted in ignoring their government. In the great capital of Edo (now Tokyo), lavish restaurants served the most sumptuous feasts, theater-going continued from morning to late at night, and the best ukiyo-e artists were hired to paint billboards for the entertainment industry. Within the green houses (the halls of carnal pleasure), where fortunes could be squandered, reigned the celebrated beauties of the day immortalized in the prints of Utamaro.

Personal vanities found expression in such baubles as inros and netsukes, on which nowadays collectors at the international auctions of Sotheby and Christie bid into the thousands. They are, of course, worth the money because no human ingenuity, time, or workmanship was spared on these small items. Indeed, no well-to-do Japanese merchant of Edo would have felt at ease at a sake-drinking party sitting next to a friend wearing a netsuke or inro of the same design. Even the Samurai class were not free from this pervading hedonism—their sword guards inlaid with intricate designs of gold, silver, and cloisonné were freely presented as gifts, but were never meant to see action in battle.

The nation was closed off from the outside world for a long time by the same ruling military dictatorship, in order to avoid seditious foreign influence such as the Christian religion. And, undisturbed by internal warfare, Japan enjoyed peace and affluence unmatched in any previous period of her history. There was an insatiable demand for arts and crafts—particularly the decorative type. This demand came from both the ruling class and the rich merchants, who were considered to be low on the social scale but had money to lend to the retainers of the noble families. Lacquer was incontestably the favorite means of decoration, equally appreciated on massive screens in the castles of the nobility and on small personal items of the bourgeois, such as inros, hair ornaments, letter boxes, and so on. The isolation that Japan imposed upon herself naturally promoted an inbreeding of the arts and crafts, and since lacquer was so indisputably popular, it strongly influenced the cloisonné craftsmen as well as artisans in other fields.

Cloisonné production began to increase, perhaps partly as a response to the demand for more ornate and decorative items during the late Tokugawa period. Many families (call them schools, if you will) were engaged in its manufacture. We hear of such celebrated names—among others—as the Hirata family,* which had already become famous for its exquisite cloisonné work. Another historically important name is Kaji Tsunekichi of Owari, who—in 1839—made plates and other large items that were admired by the Shogun. By the middle of the nineteenth century, many of his pupils were engaged in cloisonné manufacture. But as cloisonné articles were not often signed or marked, it is rather difficult to trace their makers.

The major innovative achievement was no doubt the breaking away from the labyrinthine diaper and floral patterns. The more enterprising workers began to exploit naturalistic themes, although conservative family workshops continued to use the traditional ones. This was the same course that had been taken by lacquer artists centuries before. Perhaps the cloisonné makers wanted to emulate lacquer artists, even to make their products look like lacquer. The previously mentioned translucent brown enamel liberally sprinkled with gold (copper or bronze filings) and a fine black both looked strikingly like lacquer and, not purely by accident, became the favorite background for most artistic Japanese cloisonné.

---

*The Hirata family served as the Shogun's maker of sword furniture from the early seventeenth century. Their cloisonné works are limited to small inlaid panels and plaques of translucent enamels walled in by gold wires. These are more of the jewelry type, rather than what we consider oriental cloisonné today—vessels, incense burners, and vases.

148. Beautiful in its simplicity, this vase is of matte brown and green. The enamels are of the Chinese type, but limited to early Japanese colors. Note the use of stiff leaf panels—another motif from the Chinese. Height 5 inches.

149. Pin tray with floral and butterfly design. The light blue ground is of very soft enamel that produces a matte surface.

150. Butterfly and floral design make a delicate naturalistic picture on this tray. There are age crackles in the dark blue enamel background. Length approx. 10 inches. Ca. 1880. *Keller & Scott, Carmel, California*

151. This tray shows a more formal floral and bird design against a light blue background. Length approx. 10 inches. Ca. 1890. *Keller & Scott, Carmel, California*

152A. The beginning of naturalistic design, which looks like lacquerwork. Enamel colors are soft and on the somber side; background, a grayish medium blue. Note that the placing of wires shows far from consummate skill. Minute pittings appear all over the surface. Bronze edge (border) of this tray has bamboo design. Ten inches x 5 inches. Second half of nineteenth century.

152B. Back view of item 152A showing the lingering early concept that close wire support is needed even in counterenameling.

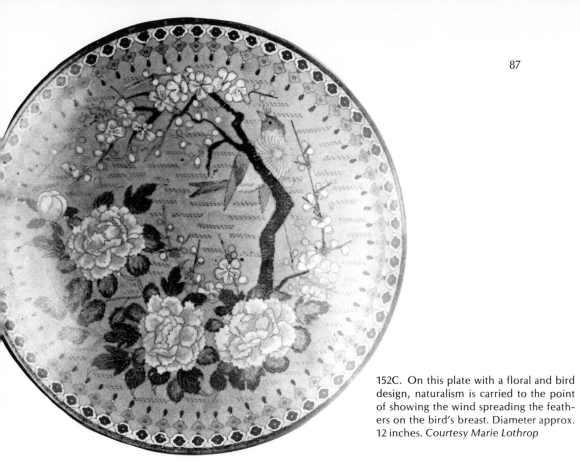

152C. On this plate with a floral and bird design, naturalism is carried to the point of showing the wind spreading the feathers on the bird's breast. Diameter approx. 12 inches. *Courtesy Marie Lothrop*

Native shapes and forms became pronounced, sometimes quaintly exaggerated. The bodies of vases were unnaturally elongated. Sometimes a ten-inch vase would stand on a tiny foot the size of a dime. The necks were tightly constricted. Jars, often divided into vertical sections, became melon-shaped, stood on three short legs, and had knobs of finely wrought bronze flowers—again, characteristically Japanese. Japanese craftsmen, perfectionists as always, knelt on their knees and worked the fine wires with tools as delicate as surgical instruments, gluing them into place according to the intricate design painted by a master designer. The glue, derived from a kind of orchid, later from a seaweed, burned away during firing without leaving the slightest discoloration. A unique Japanese style had emerged.

It is probably more rewarding, aesthetically speaking, to collect this type of cloisonné with naturalistic decoration. (See Color Plate 11.) Of course, in an oriental picture the flowers, trees, birds, insects, and fish—particularly in their interrelationships—are always more beautiful and harmonious than in nature itself, because intelligent and conscious arrangement makes them so. And flower arrangement is another important branch of oriental art. Thus, we see the wisteria vine draped around the top of the vase, with its graceful flowers cascading like a curtain; iris lines the rustic path; the gnarled pine bends down dramatically from the sky, conveniently permitting a swallow to sweep into view.

153. Jar of gray enamel with only small amount of cloisonné work composed of tiny circles around the neck and three feet. Height 3 inches; diameter 3 inches.

154. Melon-shaped covered jar on three short bronze legs. The fine decorations are divided into five sections, black and brown enamels alternating with brown enamel impregnated with gold dust. Diameter 6 inches. Ca. 1890.

155. Top view of the jar in Ill. 154. Note the finely wrought bronze flower that serves as the knob.

156. Jar with floral design on a gold-flecked brown background. The cover has a finely wrought bronze knob.

157. Vase with exquisite panels—front panel is of butterfly. Predominantly translucent brown enamel with gold dust for highlights. Height 6 inches; diameter 2½ inches. *Walter Chandoha Collection*

158. Trinket box with *mons* on dark blue background. Height 1½ inches; diameter 3 inches. *Walter Chandoha Collection*

159. Vase with elongated body, tightly constricted neck, and small foot. There are panels of pastel transparent enamels on a blue black ground. Height 11 inches; diameter at mouth 1 inch, at foot 1½ inches. *Formerly in the collection of Albert Tutino*

160. Vase decorated with two birds on the trunk of a flowering wisteria. The translucent enamel background is a very deep peacock green flecked with large and small bits of gold dust. It combines the essence of the Japanese somberness with true elegance. Height 7 inches.

162. Side view of the box in Ill. 161.

161. Hexagonal cosmetic box exquisitely decorated with flowering plants and two birds. The semi-translucent brown ground is brightened with scintillating gold specks.

163. Vase with pink peonies on a brown ground impregnated with gold dust. Height 7 inches.

164. Vase with delicate and well-arranged whitish pink peony design. Ground color is an almost indefinable soft green gray. Height 10 inches.

To meet the challenge of such designs, there had to be great technological progress. The use of enamels had to become vastly more sophisticated for the cloisonné artist to achieve the naturalistic effect. The fact that large areas of the background had to be left empty also presented technical problems. Without the support of wires to anchor the enamels and to divide the stress and tension, it was far more difficult to lay the enamels on evenly and to avoid the probable cracking after firing. Since the metal base was very thin on Japanese items, counterenameling was absolutely necessary. (This process of enameling on both sides evens up the stress and thereby strengthens the whole structure. Naturally if both sides of the object are decorated, as they are in a bowl, such a piece is counterenameled already. Where the inside of the object is not exposed to the view, as in the case of a vase, the material used is often enamel particles literally swept up from the floor of the workshop, and these result in a not-very-beautiful grayish blue or bluish black color.)

165. Tea jar with delicate light blue satiny low-gloss surface. This side bears the mallow flower. See Color Plate 14 for the opposite side with begonias.

166. Front view of a match safe from the renowned Wentworth match-safe collection.

167. Reverse of the match safe in Ill. 166.

168. Front view of another match safe from the renowned Wentworth match-safe collection. The Japanese occasionally used Egyptian motifs on their cloisonné and champlevé wares during the early 1900s.

169. Reverse of the match safe shown in Ill. 168.

170. Round covered jar with ethereal butterflies on a dark blue ground. Height 3 inches; diameter 3 inches. *Walter Chandoha Collection*

171. Yellow bowl with lotus scroll design. Height 3½ inches; diameter 8½ inches. *Walter Chandoha Collection*

172. Inside view of the bowl in Ill. 171 has an elaborate Hoo bird design. Note the use of paulownia flowers and formal chrysanthemums. *Walter Chandoha Collection*

173. Large jardiniere of fine workmanship in typical brown enamel of several shades. Som sections are brightened with specks of gold. De sign shows dragon and Hoo bird. Ca. 1900.

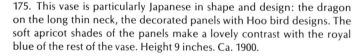

174. Reverse side of the jardiniere in Ill. 173 has a highly stylized dragon.

175. This vase is particularly Japanese in shape and design: the dragon on the long thin neck, the decorated panels with Hoo bird designs. The soft apricot shades of the panels make a lovely contrast with the royal blue of the rest of the vase. Height 9 inches. Ca. 1900.

176. Jardiniere with interesting panels decorated with designs of *mons*, eagle, and dragon. Height 8½ inches; diameter 12½ inches. *Walter Chandoha Collection*

177. Pin tray (now with added hanger) bears a design of cherry blossoms and a butterfly on a high-gloss black ground.

178. Vase with design showing a bird under chrysanthemums on a black ground. Both design and background are reminiscent of lacquerwork. Height 8 inches.

179A. Exquisite miniature vase with white iris against a black ground. Height 3½ inches.

179B. A spirited three-clawed dragon encircles this Japanese cloisonné vase. The wires are silver. Foot ring and lip ring are also silver.

180. On this vase with a black ground, the white chrysanthemums appear to be too large for the size of the vase. Height 7 inches.

The military dictatorship, even with repeated attempts, found it impossible to suppress this outburst of creative energy, particularly in the case of decorative artists and craftsmen—the ivory carvers, the metalworkers, the print artists, the actors, and naturally also the cloisonné makers. As the latter finally achieved complete mastery of their craft at the end of the Tokugawa regime, they began to seek innovation for innovation's sake. New techniques, more novelty than art, perhaps led to the decline of quality. However, the pieces made during the early 1900s do represent great strides technologically, if not artistically, and they are a variety of cloisonné that is quite readily available today.

Many of these innovations were made possible through the use of translucent and transparent enamels, which impart a jewellike appearance to the article. With this type of enamel, bits of foil could be imbedded that would act like tiny mirrors and reflect light to the viewer, thereby creating a more pleasing effect. (See Color Plate 13.) Soon the whole object was covered by reflecting silver foil with pressed patterns of dots, fish scales, waves, and other designs, similar to the basse-taille technique. Then the foil would be thickly covered by a transparent enamel of deep red (pigeon blood) or brilliant green. Against this background, the often opaque cloisonné design would stand out in contrasting but equally brilliant colors. One favorite and very effective design, for instance, was of fish swimming freely in an aquatic background consisting of a pressed pattern of waterweeds and arrowheads. It imparts an illusion of depth and movement. This is certainly eye-catching, but more and more removed from the original cloisonné technique.

183. An aquatic design on a background of intense translucent red enamel over stamped silver foil ground. (This is the so-called pigeon blood type.) The fish are in bright orange. Height 9 inches. Ca. 1930.

181. A small vase decorated in traditional style with scroll and leaf pattern in dark blue at the top has lighter blue at the bottom. Center medallion is inset with foil under peacock green enamels. Height 4 inches.

182. A traditional design decorates this vase. Bits of silver foil are embedded in the translucent enamel on the shoulder and also in the lower design. Height 8 inches.

Another procedure was to use a colorless enamel and allow the silver foil to shine through, its brightness slightly dimmed and softened. Over this liquid background, a cloisonné design in naturalistic style made with translucent enamels of pastel green and blue or lavender tones presents a subtle prettiness. When a piece of this kind suffers cracks, they show up more prominently than in the older opaque type. Dirt often lodges in the cracks and is almost impossible to cover up in repair work.

184. Vase with a bouquet of roses on a foil background, with pigeon blood translucent enamel over the background. Height 10 inches. Another available type has a slightly varied rose bouquet with deep burgundy translucent enamel.

185. Fluted dish of the pigeon blood type. Diameter 4½ inches.

186. Matching cigarette box and ashtray.

188. Earrings with rose decoration. Several pastel translucent enamels were applied to the rose and leaves. A clear transparent enamel submerges the wires, yet they are clearly visible.

187. This small jar with a deep blue green translucent ground has the same kind of rose decoration as the pieces shown in Ills. 184, 185, and 186. Ca. 1930.

189. Vase with prunus and bamboo decoration against a translucent deep blue ground over silver foil. Height 8 inches. Modern.

190. The flowers on this vase are made with delicately translucent enamels. Ground is a clear enamel over silver foil with a stamped design. Height 9 inches.

191. Vase of the same type shown in Ill. 190. The crack line on top is impossible to hide by repair work (the former owner had applied bright red fingernail polish in a big round patch!). It could at least brighten up a dark corner. Height 8 inches.

192. Vase of the same type as the two preceding ones. Goldfish and water plants create an aquatic effect. Height 4 inches.

193A. Another vase of the same type depicts cranes nesting among reeds and grasses. Height 4 inches.

193B. Bowl in the plique-à-jour cloisonné technique. Roses and buds are in shades of orange, rose, purple, and blue, between green leaves, on pale bluish green ground. Ca. 1920. *Cooper-Hewitt Museum of Design, Smithsonian Institution*

Still another type of cloisonné that uses transparent enamels is plique-à-jour. The objects are usually small bowls or small vases with wide necks. They are made by applying wires over a detachable base. The wires are attached to one another instead of to the body, using a hard solder that will not melt and discolor the enamels during the firing. When the process is completed, the base is removed—usually by an acid bath—and the light shines through from every direction. The object looks as if it were made of small pieces of stained glass. We have already mentioned that Japanese cloisonné was influenced by lacquerwork. In concept, plique-à-jour is somewhat similar to the dry lacquer technique in which the base is withdrawn after enough coats of lacquer have been applied so that the object can stand on its own. Perhaps for this reason this delicate process particularly caught the fancy of Japanese craftsmen.

This type of cloisonné is difficult to make. It is also very fragile—it can be damaged by the slightest mishap or even a sudden change of temperature. A collector friend of ours had a piece she treasured so much that it was always kept in the safest spot in her showcase. One day she dusted it carefully and put it back, but her hand slipped very slightly. The piece skidded only a couple of inches. Now it is cracked. Another collector who was a member of the armed forces during the occupation of Japan brought a piece home with him. He

194. Enamel vase. The clear outline of Mount Fuji seems to indicate that wires were used when the enamels were packed and then withdrawn before firing. The color is a cold gray blue. The smooth-surfaced enamel is very different from Chinese enamel painting, which almost always has some unevenness on the surface since the enamels are applied as they are on porcelain. Height 9 inches. Ca. 1900.

195. Cloisonné on a pottery base. The ground is bright blue. The enamels used result in a very matte surface. Ca. 1870. These pieces are scarce today.

packed it carefully with layers of soft tissue paper in a wooden box and then put the box in the center of a footlocker packed with clothing. When he got home and opened the trunk, the piece was cracked. According to him, at that time there was still one family in Japan—in fact, one woman—specializing in making this type of cloisonné. (It doesn't take a factory to make cloisonné.) When he returned to Japan, he could not find the place again.*

The Japanese also tried a unique experiment using pottery as the base for cloisonné work. The Seto potters probably started this around 1868, and Kinkou-san and others soon followed suit. However, this type of cloisonné can hardly be said to have been successful. For one thing, the pottery base necessitated that items should be fired at low temperatures and therefore very soft enamels had to be used, resulting in a matte surface easily scratched and worn. The brilliancy that is one of the beautiful features of cloisonné could not be achieved. These items often show the clumsy shapes and forms and the dull and uninteresting decorations of early Japanese cloisonné work. Under-

*Recently, bowls and vases of the plique-à-jour type have again become available. The design seems to be limited to sprays of roses and leaves, which form a good framework for the enamels. Because of their fragility, makers refuse to ship these pieces. Buyers must get them from Japan on their own, and the price is high —from $200 up.

standably, the making of ceramic-based cloisonné was slowly but surely discontinued, and such pieces have become scarce and very high priced in recent years. (See Color Plate 14.)

There are other techniques also worth mentioning: some cloisonné was begun in the standard way, but after the enamels were filled in, the wires were withdrawn before firing. This is called "wireless cloisonné." In another type of work, transparent enamels were applied not only in the cells but over the wires. These techniques were meant to give a softer effect.

Japanese cloisonné reached its peak of magnificence by the late nineteenth century, but in the meantime it had also sown the seeds of its own decline. Cherry blossoms and many other Japanese things are at their best when they are fading. So it was with Japanese cloisonné. Articles continued to be made in this medium, but in larger numbers and with an eye to the export market. They are only mockeries of their predecessors. Cloisonné works were even attempted by partly filling the cells with lacquer instead of enamel. Coincidentally, Mr. R. H. Leary, in his recent investigation of the cloisonné articles in the Palace Museum on Taiwan, reported that there are a few Chinese items made by the same method.

196. By definition, this vase should belong to the cloisonné category. The base is pottery, and a coat of thick stippled material was applied over it. Next, a fine cloisonné work of bronze wires was attached (note the dragon on the body and the decorations on both the neck and foot). Finally, the cells were filled with multicolored (olive green, dark green, orange, and red) lacquers. The cloisonné work was never fired; the dragon and the other decorations were simply smoothed and left with a silky matte surface.

197. A stock design of a bouquet of roses on an opaque pastel yellow ground. Height 8 inches.

Japan ended her isolation in 1854 and her medieval feudal government in 1868. In less than half a century, by taking the West as her model, she was able to emerge as a modern country. She defeated Russia and China and annexed Korea. In this headlong rush, however, she achieved her coveted big-power status among the family of nations at the expense of her arts and crafts, in which she had been preeminent—among them, the art of making exquisite cloisonné.

Cloisonné objects became nothing but sterile repetitions of one or two stock designs: a patch of decoration consisting of either a bird sitting on a stiff branch of blooming prunus or cherry and utterly devoid of oriental charm, or a bouquet of roses that looks more Western than a Western still life in oils. This small patch of cloisonné work, so exactly alike piece after piece as to appear machine-stamped, was then planted over a pressed silver foil that was smoothly covered by a transparent enamel of either red or green or, for variation, over pastel-colored opaque enamels (of course without the foil). To be sure, even such delicate work as plique-à-jour was made in limited quantity down to the 1930s. But such tours de force really represent technical virtuosity rather than artistic excellence.

All such modern objects are limited as to shape and form; usually they are squat jars, vases, cigarette boxes, or jewelry (earrings, necklaces, bracelets). They are heavy and sturdy, and the metal rings on the neck and foot of the vessels are chrome-bright. Sometimes the label "Japan" or "Made in Japan" is stamped on the foot rim. A six-inch vase of this type (they are still being made) just imported into the United States retails now for about $70.

198. Another stock design. The ground is a pastel yellow. Height 9 inches.

199. Modern vase with bright cerise sweet peas on a green vine, butterflies, and a light blue gray ground. Decoration appears on one side only. Height 9 inches.

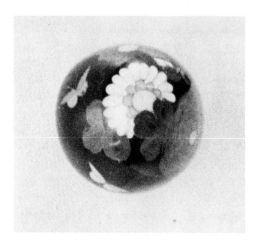

200. Sphere with two stylized chrysanthemums and two butterflies on a dark blue ground. The threaded hole in one end shows it was originally from a lady's hairpin. The workmanship is exquisite. Diameter 1 inch. Ca. 1880.

201. Another sphere, this one covered by a close pattern of prunus blossoms, made in the same manner as the sphere in Ill. 200. Diameter, less than one inch. Ca. 1880.

202. Shichiho Inaba, Sr., founder of the Inaba cloisonné firm.

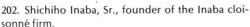

203. Shichiho Inaba, Jr., son of the founder.

Off the beaten track, nonetheless, are still a few hardy souls who want to keep alive their proud family tradition of fine workmanship that has been preserved for several generations. Recently, the editors of *Arts of Asia*, a Hong Kong magazine that is fast becoming one of the most important in the field of oriental art, paid a visit to the Inaba cloisonné workshop founded in 1887 by the father of the present owner, Shichiho Inaba, Jr.* We are very grateful to *Arts of Asia* and its editors for permission to reproduce the pictures showing the actual stages of the original technique by which cloisonné was made many years ago and is made in the Inaba shop even today.

*Tuyet Nguyet, and R.H. Leary, "Inaba Cloisonné," *Arts of Asia*, Vol. 3, No. 5, Sept.-Oct. 1973.

204. The Inaba shop on Sanjo east of Higashioji, not far from the Miyako Hotel.

205. Beating the metal ground into the required shape.

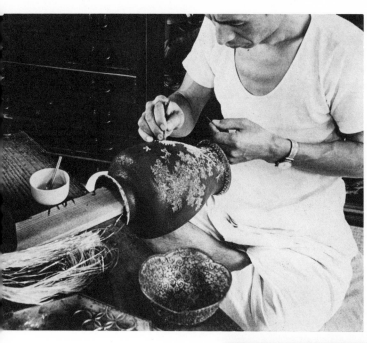

206. Lining out the design with fine metal wires.

207. Bowl with completed design, ready to take the enamel.

208. Applying the enamels.

209. Box going into the muffle.

210. Vase coming out of the charcoal furnace.

211. In the final stages—hand-polishing.

212. Long-necked vase ($1300 in American currency).

9

Marks,
Symbols,
and Motifs

ALMOST EVERY ORIENTAL OBJECT SEEMS an entrancing mystery because it is thought (and rightfully so) that the unfamiliar markings or decorations have hidden meanings. Also, the written characters of the Far East are incomprehensible to most Westerners who have not given long tedious hours over a period of many years to studying their pictorial origin. However, an understanding of the frequently used and thoroughly fascinating symbols of China and Japan can be quite readily achieved.

Realizing this, we will illustrate and explain some of the meanings not only of the ideographs but of the symbols and decorations used by the Chinese. The Japanese later copied and modified these, as well as creating some of their own. Together, all these form an oriental symbolic language.

Only a few marks (either reign marks or those of the craftsmen) need be

113

illustrated because most cloisonné was not marked. Even Japanese workmen, contrary to their tradition, rarely signed their pieces. The reason may have been that the artists employed in the cloisonné ateliers were under the patronage of certain daimyos (feudal lords) for whose exclusive use the objects were made—therefore, signatures were unnecessary. Later on, when the export trade began, signed pieces still occurred only rarely—probably because many hands were employed in making a single piece and, too, the workshops may not have achieved the kind of status enjoyed by the lacquer and pottery artists.

5. Period
6. Made

3. K'ang-
4. hsi (1662-1722)

1. Great
2. Ch'ing
(1644-1912)

5. Period
6. Made

3. Hsüan-
4. te

1. Great
2. Ming
(1368-1644)

3. Yung-
4. cheng
(1723-1735)

3. Ching-
4. t'ai
(1450-1457)

3. Ch'ien
4. lung
(1736-1795)

3. Chia-
4. ching
(1522-1566)

Fig. 1A. Reign marks on cloisonné. Collectors need learn only the characters numbered 3 and 4 in each period.

3. Wan-
4. li
(1573-1619)

The Chinese used only half a dozen or so reign marks on cloisonné, and these were made an integral part of the body through the use of the cloisons and enamels and, of course, casting. (Those incised on the base are often suspect.) Only the finest specimens were marked in this way. Pieces for export sometimes had "China" or "Made in China" enameled on the base of the object—with or without the benefit of wires. These, plus a few makers' marks, are all that need be represented.

JAPANESE

平
田

Hirata family

CHINESE

達
古
齋

Ta Ku Tsai

洋
天
利

Yang T'ien Lee

老
天
利

Lao T'ien Lee

Fig. 1B. Makers' marks

THE GREAT T'AO-T'IEH MASK AND OTHER ARCHAIC SYMBOLS

"They managed to get it all together!" Dare we use such an expression in discussing the *t'ao-t'ieh* mask? And what did they get all together? The Shang peoples came to a single totem representation on the bronzes they cast at least as long ago as 1,500 years before the Christian era. Their bird worship shows up in the clawed foot. The mammalian and serpent totem reveals itself on each side with a C-shaped horn, an elongated curled tail, and a body that becomes the sum of the other parts without a noticeable main section. If one blocks out half the illustration of the entire motif, the profile of the creature is apparent.

Fig. 2. The *t'ao-t'ieh* Mask

To the occidental, this mask looks as if it might have been worn over the eyes as a means of scaring away evil spirits or fooling other people by concealing one's identity. Of course the Shang (or the Chou) peoples never wore this sort of mask—it is merely a symbol of the worship of mythological animals and nature forms in which they engaged. Cast in bronze on their ceremonial vessels, it came to symbolize gluttony (possibly because early Chinese writers identified it as the gluttonous monster), but its entire significance is still not absolutely certain. Recent studies of the bronze pieces in the possession of the National Palace Museum in Taiwan seem to suggest that the original representation may have been that of the beloved water buffalo. Certainly this would give a different significance to the meaning of the mask. And since the Chinese had long depended upon the water buffalo for the heavy farm work, it is reasonable to believe that they might turn to it for a totem or part of one. Anthropologists might also point out that it could have represented their turning away from a nomadic tribal existence to a stationary farm community.

Whatever its origin and purpose, this mask was uncommon as a decoration on cloisonné until the Ch'ing dynasty during the Ch'ien-lung reign (1736-1785). At that time it was a popular tendency to combine the shape, form, and decor of archaic bronze with the cloisonné art, and the *t'ao-t'ieh* motif was thus freely adapted into the decorative scheme of cloisonné.

The archaic dragon is thought to be as old as the mask. It is sometimes found as part of the decoration on cloisonné and was often used in the form of cast-bronze handles on many large pieces.

Fig. 3. Archaic dragons

The mythical rooster, *t'ien-chi*, also seems to have developed from the archaic bird motif used on bronze. It is likely to be found as a whole cloisonné piece complete with a sacrificial cup on its back. The *t'ien-chi* may have been the forerunner of the phoenix and the Japanese Hoo bird.

Fig. 4. The archaic bird

Through centuries of cultural additions, with ethics, religion, and superstition making contributions to the symbolic language of the people, the dragon —the most important Chinese national symbol, in fact—underwent many evolutional changes. From the one-footed *kuei* of the Shang and Chou dynasties it evolved into a four-footed creature with or without rudimentary horns.

By the thirteenth or fourteenth century, the elaborate dragon appeared complete with flames, scales, antelopelike horns, and a beautiful tail, plus claws—three in the early days (and still so made by the Japanese) and later four for high officials and five for the emperor. By K'ang-hsi's reign (1662-1722), the dragon appeared with flowing mane and whiskers, worthy of the majesty and magnificence of the Middle Kingdom and its ruler. It was depicted chasing the flaming pearl symbolizing treasure, enlightenment, or any highly sought gift or accomplishment.

Another form of the dragon (perhaps the result of Buddhist influence) often has a foliated tail, an elephant nose (short trunk), and frequently a stalk of flowers (lotus) emerging from its mouth.

Fig. 5A. Chinese dragon

Fig. 5B. Dragon showing Buddhist influence

Following the dragon, or perhaps developing simultaneously, was the phoenix in all of its beauty. Many pieces of cloisonné have a phoenix on one side and a dragon on the other, representing male-female, emperor-empress, god-goddess, or the happy balance of yang and yin or yin and yang.

Fig. 6. Phoenix

Another form that should be seen as part of early semireligious symbolism is the *ch'i-lin* or unicorn. The *ch'i-lin*, a mythical creature found whenever a sage emperor or philosopher was born, is often depicted on artifacts as carrying the emperor on its back or carrying Confucius; it was said that a *ch'i-lin* appeared when Confucius was born. The story is told that in the hope of pleasing a Ming emperor, a live *ch'i-lin* was sought, and the search resulted in the emperor's being presented with an actual live giraffe!

Fig. 7. *Ch'i-lin*

Although the *ch'i-lin* is often confused with the Fo dog or lion, he should be depicted as having the body of a deer, the hoof of a horse, the tail of an ox, and a head like the dragon, except that in the earliest version he had a single horn. He is said to be so gentle and graceful that he could walk through the world without stepping on even the smallest living creature.

SYMBOLS OF THE UNIVERSE

Perhaps the most fascinating and the most meaningful symbol of China is the yin-yang surrounded by the Eight Trigrams (*pa kua*), considered to be the earliest form of Chinese writing. Together these, when fully expounded, explain the very essence of the creation: life and its meaning. The yin-yang or the yang-yin has to do with the pulsating rhythm of the universe. It is often thought of in terms of the male-female, but within that concept lies the realization that at times, within the yang (male), the yin (female) is uppermost in activity; conversely, within the yin (female), the yang (male) is sometimes dominant. In other words, the weak pulse and the strong pulse move in harmony within all things. When they are off balance, something goes wrong. If this occurs within the individual, a disorder will result—an illness or an unhappiness. If the imbalance is within the ruler's being, he or she may cause disharmony among the people. If the disharmony is within nature, there will come floods, drought, earthquakes, and other natural disasters.

Fig. 8. *Pa kua*

The Eight Trigrams surrounding the yin-yang also have esoteric meaning. They represent heaven, earth, and other important elements. They can, in combination, be made to explain the basic principles of the universe. When arranged in threes and fours (the plain and broken lines), they can have an almost infinite number of meanings. These were explained first in the famous *I Ching* (*Book of Changes*). When one sees the Eight Trigrams surrounding the yin-yang sign on any object, it is a super good-luck symbol.

From this all-pervading principle of yin-yang interacting with nature, artistic motifs such as clouds, earth, rocks, mountains, and waves have acquired majestic meanings. They appear on the emperor's dragon robe. They are also very common on cloisonné pieces.

Fire

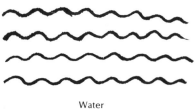

Water

Clouds

Waves

Rocks

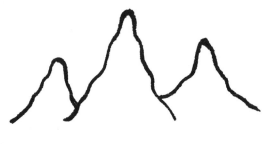

Mountains

Fig. 9.

Fig. 10. Stylized mountain, sea, and waves symbolize the emperor's rule over the whole domain. This theme always appears on the emperor's robes. Westerners call it the "Rock of Ages."

REBUSES AND FREQUENT IDEOGRAPHS

The rebus mode of expression was particularly popular during the late Ming and through the Ch'ing dynasties. Figures 11 through 14 show the most familiar and most frequently used ones. Not only the double rebus but also a triple rebus is common.

Fig. 11. *Fu* means "good fortune" or "bat" when vocalized. Thus the picture of the bat is used to denote good fortune.

Fig. 12A. *Lu*, when pronounced, means either "high position" or "deer," and a deer used in decoration therefore signifies "high position."

Fig. 12B. *Suan* and *Chien* (the double coin) when vocalized can also mean "both complete." When this symbol is combined with the bat (*Fu*) and the deer (*Lu*), the meaning is: Complete with both good fortune and high position.

Fig. 13. *Kwei*, when pronounced, means "nobility" or the "cassia flower." (The cassia is an evergreen with beautiful leaves and clusters of small yellow flowers that have a delightful fragrance.) When the cassia flower is part of the decoration on a piece, it denotes "nobility."

Fig. 14. More complicated is the triple rebus. For instance, *pi* (a brush) and *t'ing* (a silver or gold ingot), when put together, can mean "will certainly be." *Ju yi* is a wand with a mushroomlike head carried by a man of prestige, but it can also mean "as you wish." When all three of these appear together in a group, the overall meaning is "Everything will certainly happen as you wish." A birthday gift wrapped in a paper with these symbols on it indicated the donor was saying: "All your birthday wishes will come true."

Also frequently seen on Chinese objects are the "happiness" and "double happiness" characters (Figs. 15 and 16). They refer to happiness in marriage or conjugal bliss.

The *shou* character, another well-known Chinese symbol, means longevity. Actually, it can be written in a hundred different forms, some of which are shown in Figure 17.

喜

Fig. 15. Happiness

Fig. 16. Double happiness

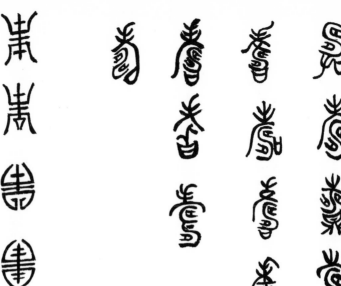

Fig. 17.

A few of the hundred ways
to write "longevity"

Most frequently seen
longevity characters

Less frequently seen
longevity characters

213A. Reverse side of the painted
enamel stack dishes shown in Ill. 29.
Each of the four dishes bears the
"double happiness" character. This
item, therefore, must have been intended for a bride's trousseau.

213B. Painted enamel tray showing favorite motifs—
"five bats" surrounding the *shou* character. Combined,
these mean five kinds of good luck and longevity too.
The translucent enamel is over a silvered copper repoussé base. Diameter 3½ inches.

The twelve zodiac symbols are less frequently seen on cloisonné, but the first is always the rat because, according to the folk story, it was to the rat that, after Creation, Heaven gave the job of naming the symbols of the zodiac. He ran bragging to his uncle, the cat, that he had been chosen for this very important task.

"That is very good, my dear nephew. Now don't forget me, your old uncle," said the cat. "Be sure to give me a place in the zodiac."

"Oh, no, good uncle, I promise not to forget you," replied the rat, and he went out to select animal friends to represent the twelve posts. Every animal begged the rat for the honor of being chosen.

First the rat named himself, then the cow, the tiger, the hare, dragon, serpent, horse, ram, monkey, cock, dog, and pig. Finally, exhausted, he returned home. At once the uncle asked if he had been included among the twelve, as promised. The rat, greatly embarrassed but unable to do anything about it since he had already sent the list to Heaven, was forced to answer: "Oh, dear, dear uncle, I forgot."

"I'll murder you," yelled the cat, and he set out after his fleeing nephew. From that day on the cat has never forgiven his erstwhile relative, the rat.

Fig. 18. The zodiac

CONFUCIANISM, TAOISM, BUDDHISM

The conventional way of presenting oriental symbols (particularly Chinese symbols) is to divide them into Confucian (literati), Taoist, and Buddhist; we will follow that convention. Not everything, however, falls neatly into these categories because they do overlap, and probably many of the symbols were derived from other sources—medicine, astrology, astronomy, and agriculture. Another way of explaining the difference is to say that most Confucian symbols have to do with the order of society, the family, and government. Most of the Taoist symbols, on the other hand, derive from the love of nature and natural phenomena and a state of being called immortality; most Buddhist symbols have a religious meaning, such as enlightenment and eternal happiness. Having said this, we still must repeat that there is no clear-cut separation of these three elements.

First, the Confucian or literati symbols: the four accomplishments or four treasures of the gentleman-scholar were considered to be the lute, chess game, books, and painting scrolls. These represented the most indispensable endeavors of the scholar.

Fig. 19. The lute, the first of the four literati symbols

Fig. 20. The chess game, the second literati symbol. Adopted by the Japanese, it is called go in their language.

Fig. 21. The third literati symbol: the books

Fig. 22. Scrolls of painting, the fourth literati symbol

Also closely connected with the scholastic tradition are the "hundred antiques." These are the many types of antique bronze censers and porcelain vases (often with the addition of sprays of prunus or other blossoms). Also on the scholar's table would be such items as the ink stick, ink box, ink stone, a brush holder, and water coupe (or sometimes a water dropper). All were part and parcel of the accouterments of the gentleman-scholar, but used as decorations as well, to give the object so decorated affinity with the literati.

Fig. 23. Examples of the "hundred antiques"

The "Eight Precious or Eight Ordinary Symbols," which came from various traditional native Chinese sources, had been accumulating since ancient times. They were accepted by all regardless of their religious beliefs.

Fig. 24. The sonorous stone (jade). Used as a bell, it symbolizes good judgment. It is also an emblem of good luck.

Fig. 25. The pair of books, the emblem of learning, also is a charm against evil spirits.

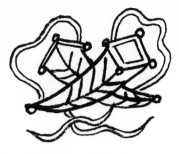

Fig. 26. The pair of rhinoceros horns carved to represent drinking cups symbolize happiness—possibly conjugal happiness.

Fig. 27. The artemisia leaf, another symbol of happiness, is also a charm to cure illness. In fact, this leaf is actually used as a curative by herb doctors.

Fig. 28. The pearl, a charm against fire, flood, and other disasters, also denotes feminine purity and beauty.

Fig. 29. The coin is an emblem of wealth.

Fig. 30. The mirror is both a symbol of conjugal felicity and a charm to ward off evil spirits.

Fig. 31. The lozenge, an ancient musical instrument, symbolizes victory and achievement.

Lao-tzu, who lived about the same time as Confucius, was considered to be the founder of Taoism. With Taoism, or rather the religion of Taoism, which came later, a whole new world of symbolism and folklore arose.

The supreme rulers of Taoist Heaven are the Queen Mother of the West and her consort the Emperor of the East. Next in rank in the hierarchy are the three stars or the three gods. The first is *Fu*, or good luck, who is often represented with a baby boy in his arms. The second is the star of high rank, *Lu*, shown in the costume of a high official with a scepter in his hand; and, finally, *Shou* is the star of longevity, the familiar figure of exaggerated head with a staff and a peach. When all three stars smile upon a person, he is fortunate indeed.

The Eight Immortals or *pa hsien* are believed to be actual persons who attained the state of immortality. They can be easily recognized by the symbolic objects they carry. They are supposed to represent the eight conditions of life:* masculinity and feminity, poverty and wealth, age and youth, intellectual accomplishment and detachment from it.

THE EIGHT TAOIST SYMBOLS

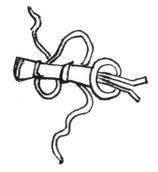

Fig. 32. The Fan of Han Chung-li, the first of the eight Taoist symbols

Fig. 33. The second Taoist symbol, the Bamboo Tube of Chang Kuo-lao

Fig. 34. The Sword of Lü Tung-pin

*The Japanese adopted these symbols as decorations without necessarily referring to the immortals. People often equate the Japanese Seven Gods of Fortune with the Eight Immortals. They are different, and their symbols are very different from the eight Taoist symbols.

Fig. 35. The Castanets of Ts'ao Kuo-chiu

Fig. 36. The Gourd and Iron Crutch of Li T'ieh-kuai are the fifth Taoist symbol.

Fig. 37. Han Hsiang-tzu's Flute is the sixth Taoist symbol.

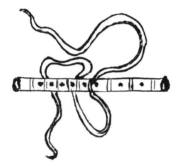

Fig. 38. The Lotus Blossom and Seed-pod of Ho Hsien-ku

Fig. 39. The eighth Taoist symbol is the Basket of Flowers of Lan Ts'ai-ho.

Chief of the immortals is Han Chung-li, who was said to have used his fan to revive the souls of the dead. It seems that Han Chung-li came upon a woman kneeling at a grave and passionately fanning it. When Han Chung-li asked her why she was doing such a thing, she said that when her husband was dying he had begged her to wait until the soil around his grave was dry before she married again. Now it had so happened that very shortly after her husband's death she met a man she wanted to marry, and so, since her husband's grave was still damp, she was trying to blow it dry with her fan.

Han Chung-li felt sorry for her. He took her fan and struck the grave with it, and the earth immediately became dry. The grateful woman insisted that he keep the fan as a reward.

Han Chung-li took the fan home with him, and his own wife immediately asked about it. When he told her the story, she became incensed at the woman and vowed that she herself would never behave in such a shameful way. Deciding to test her, Han Chung-li pretended to be dead. She buried him. Then he turned himself into a handsome young suitor and came to court her.

Within a few days she had agreed to marry the young man, who promptly told her he needed her first husband's brains to concoct a potion that would give them eternal youth. She agreed to open the grave for him, and when she did, Han Chung-li raised himself out of it. She was so humiliated that she went home and hanged herself. Han Chung-li burned their house and walked away with only the fan, which he carried ever after.

The second immortal is Chang Kuo-lao, the magician often depicted riding a mule backward. He was supposed to be able to fold up his mule like a piece of paper and put it in a bag when he did not need it. Chang Kuo-lao is always shown with a bamboo tube containing a bundle of rods.

Lü Tung-pin, the third immortal, is usually shown carrying a fly whisk and a sword. The fly whisk is often considered a symbol of both Taoism and Buddhism because their believers do not like to kill living creatures—they can shoo flies away with the whisk. The sword is also an appropriate emblem for him because he went about the world for four hundred years vanquishing evil wherever he saw it.

Ts'ao Kuo-chiu, the fourth immortal, merited the robes of high office that he wore because his father was a military commander and his sister a queen during the Sung dynasty. He was the patron saint of theater actors, and therefore carries castanets.

Li T'ieh-kuai, the fifth immortal, is shown with the iron crutch. He, meaning his soul, after having taken a long journey over the mountains and seas in the manner of the immortals, failed to return to his body at the appointed hour, and his disciple, thinking him dead, burned the body. When Li returned to this life, he had to enter the corpse of a crippled beggar. He carries a pilgrim's gourd, which is believed to possess great magical power, and the beggar's iron crutch.

Han Hsiang-tzu, the patron saint of musicians and the sixth immortal, has the flute as his emblem. He saved the life of his uncle, the great T'ang dynasty statesman and scholar Han Yu, who was unjustly ostracized by the emperor.

Ho Hsien-ku, the seventh immortal, wandered through the forest finding bamboo shoots for her sick mother, but she herself needed no food and could live on powdered mother-of-pearl and moonbeams. Her special province is the home, and she carries the lotus blossom and lotus seedpod.

Lan Ts'ai-ho has threadbare garments and only one shoe. This patron saint of gardeners, the eighth immortal, carries a basket of flowers.

There are other Taoist folk figures. The boy with a string of gold coins and a three-legged toad, a good luck symbol, is one of the lesser characters. The twin genii of harmony, Ho-Hu, are often seen on lacquer, wood, pottery, and porcelain, and sometimes on cloisonné; most are statuettes.

214. Painted enamel tray that illustrates the story of the boy, a minor Taoist figure, who fished out the magic three-legged toad with a gold coin. The painting is poor and the artist (a Chinese feminist?) depicted a girl instead of a boy.

Buddhism came to China at just the right moment in history to be accepted, and it spread throughout the land within a short time. It flourished during the Southern and Northern dynasties (265-581) when there was much conquest and slaughter by the barbaric tribes. The people were in deep misery, and Buddhism, a true religion, promised salvation. It was not long before still another symbolic language had become a part of Chinese and, later, Japanese life.

215. Painted enamel box decorated with "the four treasures of the scholar's studio," or "the four accomplishments." The border is repoussé in bronze showing the Buddhist symbols.

"The Eight Happy Omens of Buddhism" represent a mixture of Buddhist and traditional Chinese values. Incidentally, it should be mentioned here that when oriental symbols are shown with ribbons attached to them, the ribbons endow the objects with supernatural powers (they also make for a more decorative symbol).

Fig. 40. The umbrella was the symbol for all-encompassing authority as well as shelter for all living things.

Fig. 41. The canopy was to be held high during important ceremonial rites or processions.

Fig. 42. The third "Happy Omen of Buddhism," the Conch Shell, when put to the ear enabled one to hear the Buddha's voice giving counsel.

Fig. 43. The Everlasting Knot is the fourth "Happy Omen." This particular weaving or type of knot can be continued on and on, just as life goes on and on, a continuous renewal. Because it has eight endings, it symbolizes the Eight Admonitions of the Buddha: "Do not kill, do not steal, do not fornicate, do not bear false witness, and do not drink wine" were the first five; the last three had to do with life in old age, patience in sickness, and preparing for death. The everlasting knot is also a symbol of everlasting happiness.

Fig. 44. The Wheel of Law is the symbol of truth and the life of the Buddha himself. It carries with it the meaning that superstitions can be overcome—it has the power to destroy them.

Fig. 45. The sixth "Happy Omen," the Lotus Flower, is the symbol of purity and perfection. It has the power to overcome the mud from which it arises; hence, it signifies man's ability to rise above the contamination of the world.

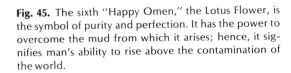

Fig. 46. The Double Fish was the symbol of conjugal faithfulness, fertility, and plenty.

Fig. 47. The Covered Jar, the eighth "Happy Omen," represents the Buddhist belief in overcoming death. The jar was used for the ashes of the priests.

FLOWERS, FRUIT, TREES, BAMBOO, AND FUNGUS

Oriental peoples have a deep and abiding love for flowers and plant life. To represent these in painting constitutes one highly regarded specialty of art. It is therefore quite natural that floral patterns became the most prominent theme in the decoration of cloisonné. Among the more popular flowers were the magnolia, cassia, prunus (Chinese plum) blossoms, lotus, orchid, peony, rose, chrysanthemum, wisteria, iris, and cherry; the last four were and are especially beloved by the Japanese. The four with particular symbolic meaning are the prunus, orchid, bamboo, and chrysanthemum, known as the "Four Gentlemen." The bamboo ranks high with the Chinese; it was included with the "Four Gentlemen" even though it is not, strictly speaking, a flower. It is also included with the "Three Friends of Winter"—the pine, bamboo, and prunus —there is a connotation that these three represent Confucius (bamboo), Buddha (pine), and Lao-tzu (prunus).

216. Two painted-enamel dishes decorated with "hundred antiques" motif and a variety of favorite Chinese plants and fruits.

217A. A large Chinese painted-enamel peach that serves no purpose except as a decoration, to remind one of the peach of "longevity."

217B. Three Chinese pin trays of silver-gilded copper repoussé covered by translucent green enamel. The peaches have faint minute specks of red shading into bright tips.

218. Painted enamel tray with pomegranates and blossoms on a white ground. Diameter 7 inches.

Fig. 48. "The Four Gentlemen"

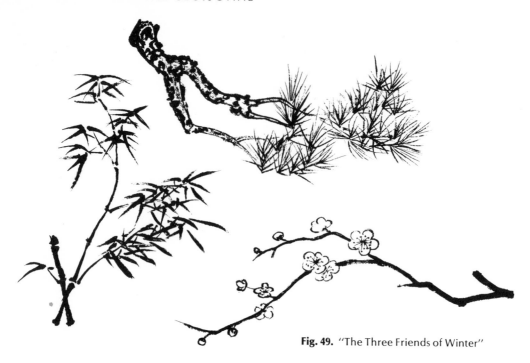

Fig. 49. "The Three Friends of Winter"

The peony and rose are symbols of affluence. The lotus in its stylized form (the so-called Indian lotus scroll) has been the most popular design since the beginning of cloisonné work in the early Ming dynasty.

One of the most frequently used designs is a series of stiff leaves. Included in this broad group are the following: 1) those on the Shang and Chou bronzes with archaic designs, which are often called the cicada motif; 2) an elongated, slender banana leaf; 3) the lotus petal. The first two are the kind used on the slender neck of a vessel—either pointing up or downward. The lotus petal is more appropriate for a short wide foot.

The peach has special significance as the Taoist symbol of longevity. It is a food fit for the immortals. At the feast given by the Taoist Queen Mother of the West, according to Chinese legend, the peach was served as the main attraction of the gathering. The God of Longevity (with exaggerated head) is always represented holding a peach in his hand.

The lotus blossom is a symbol of purity because, although it rises out of the mud on a lake bottom, it blooms with brilliance and purity. The pod may be used as a symbol of many offspring, the same symbolic meaning as conveyed by the beautiful pomegranate when it opens to reveal its numerous red seeds.

As a symbol of immortality the Chinese also used the sacred fungus (*ling-chi*) or mushroom because, after it dries, it seems to last forever. The sacred fungus has as many as nine branches.

The Buddha's-hand citron is to be seen on many porcelains and cloisonnés. The fruit, a citron, is not eaten, but as it grows it reminds one of a hand gracefully held out in a gesture of helpfulness or sympathy. Since it usually has more than five fingers, it may also indicate the many ways Buddha has of helping people.

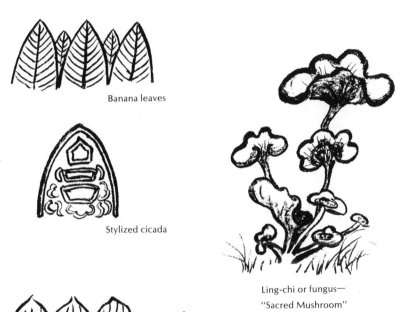

Banana leaves

Stylized cicada

Ling-chi or fungus—
"Sacred Mushroom"

Lotus petals

THREE EXAMPLES OF STIFF LEAF MOTIFS

Stylized Indian lotus scroll

Buddha's-hand citron

Double gourd

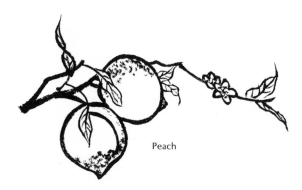

Peach

Pomegranate

The double gourd has been mentioned as a pilgrim's symbol. The gourd in and of itself is such a pleasingly artistic object that, not surprisingly, it is used as a decoration or in sculptural form. To the Taoist, it symbolizes a container for elixir, a drink with special curative properties.

Certain trees were also meaningful to the oriental people. The pine stands for durability, the willow for both strength and pliability. The pine was often used by both the Chinese and Japanese along with the crane, another Taoist symbol for longevity, since the crane is known to be long-lived. (The tortoise was also a symbol for longevity, and the crane was often depicted riding on its back. A branch of pine is invariably a part of a painting of these two.) The lichi, a delicious juicy fruit that grows in clusters, again may symbolize many offspring.

BIRDS, INSECTS, AND FISH

What other animal but the duck, particularly the wood duck, could so well represent conjugal happiness and love? Both the Chinese and Japanese employ ducks, in pairs, in decoration. Other birds found on cloisonné are the cock, which heralds the beginning of day and therefore stands for diligence; the swallow, the sign of spring; the sparrow, to represent a large clan; the hawk, the sign of strength; the peacock, to depict elegance and beauty; and the magpie, a bringer of happy news.

Fish—the golden carp and the elaborate fan-tailed—are never forgotten by the oriental artist. Insects are an integral part of life, as can be seen in the decorative schemes that are used. Where flowers are pictured there are also often insects to give the plants the added interest of life, so to speak. The cricket, butterfly, cicada (an ancient symbol of resurrection), and the katydid are among the favored insects.

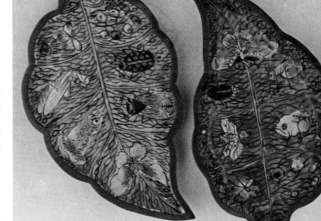

219. Leaf-shaped painted-enamel trays in bright green and other gay colors. Depicted on them are insects, a butterfly, three-legged toad, frog, lichi fruit, and lotus blossoms.

ANIMALS

Animals are often part of the decoration on cloisonné, but they also appear as figural specimens, cast or sculptured in copper or bronze and covered with cloisonné work in various forms of diaper patterns.

The Eight Horses of the Emperor Mu Wang of the Chou dynasty, so often shown in other art media, are rarely found in cloisonné, but the lucky seeker may find a box or lily bowl with them as part of the design. The tortoise, which signifies longevity, as mentioned before, can be seen as a part of cloisonné decoration too. (The Japanese tortoise has a wide featherlike tail.) The "hare on the moon" compounds an elixir (at the behest of the moon goddess); the hare also symbolizes longevity. Almost any animal can be found as a part of cloisonné decoration, but the Chinese have been especially talented in making figures of them (in the round). Among those most popular were ducks, archaic birds, Fo dogs, frogs, hares, horses, deer, quail, cranes, and water buffalo; even a child on a hobbyhorse was a favorite figure of the early Ch'ing era. A cloisonné incense burner in the form of a unicorn was a popular piece of the eighteenth century.

Fo dogs, originally a representation of the lions that guarded the Buddhist temples, were reproduced by the Chinese. After several centuries of changes and modifications, the lions began to look more like Pekinese dogs and to seem like playful creatures. As decorations, the one is sometimes shown as playing with a ball (male) and the other gently playing with a puppy (female).

* * * * *

JAPANESE SYMBOLS

The Japanese cloisonnés were frequently decorated with the aforementioned Chinese motifs, but the Japanese had many that were exclusively their own. Very few if any of these strictly Japanese motifs are ever found on Chinese works.

First to be mentioned are the iris and wisteria—flowers beloved by the Japanese and beautifully depicted by them in every form of art. The brilliant autumn maple leaf is also a persistent Japanese motif.

The *mon* or crest was originally a personal emblem. However, *mons* have come to be used purely as decorations. The two that have (and still have today) an important meaning are the sixteen-petal chrysanthemum of the stylized type called the *Kiku no mon* and the paulownia flower and its leaves in their many forms, the *Kiri no mon*. The chrysanthemum represents the emperor and the paulownia plant represents the empress. If one is confronted with any artwork bearing either of these symbols, he can be sure it is Japanese (although some forms of stylized chrysanthemums may be found among other flowers on Chinese pieces).

Fig. 51A. Japanese decorations

"Kiku no mon"

"Kiri no mon"

Examples of "mons" found on cloisonné

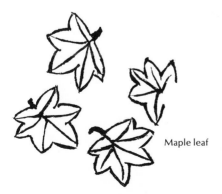

Maple leaf

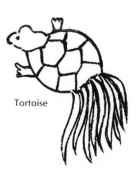

Tortoise

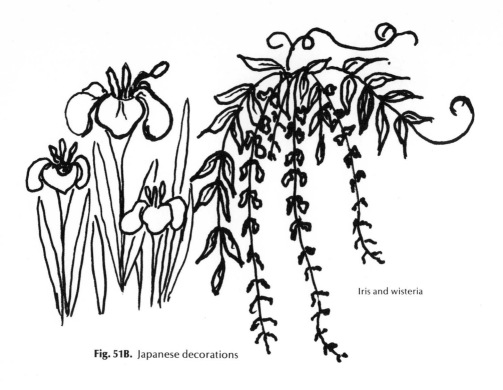

Iris and wisteria

Fig. 51B. Japanese decorations

STYLIZED MOTIFS OR DIAPER PATTERNS

The diaper pattern is an overall design that is both decorative and functional. In the beginning, the diaper was employed on cloisonné work as a means of keeping the enamels in place and breaking up the stress in open areas to prevent cracking. The Chinese have rarely abandoned the diaper pattern, except in pieces that have sufficient design to hold the enamels in place. In the later years when the enamels were easier to handle, the Chinese made a few pieces without the use of the extra wiring. The Japanese, however, in the late nineteenth century did use wide expanses of thick enamel without a diaper pattern, though their early work shows the same dependence upon extra wires. Therefore, it is not entirely true to say that the Japanese did not use diaper patterns and that the Chinese always did. Neither statement is absolutely accurate. One must look at other criteria to distinguish the two.

The diaper patterns of course have their symbolic meanings, particularly those that have acquired Western nicknames, so to speak. Take, for instance, the so-called swastika and T pattern. The oriental people call it the interlocking *wan*. (*Wan* means ten thousand.) When all the "ten thousands" are linked together, they can denote millions of years or millions of dollars (taels of gold or silver, properly speaking); therefore the *wan* diaper is a good luck symbol. Again, the cloud pattern may signify plentiful rain and therefore a good harvest. So it is with many of if not all the diaper patterns.

It would indeed be fatuous to pretend that the marks, symbols, and decorations described here are anywhere near all those used on oriental cloisonnés. Those illustrated and explained, however, are sufficient at least to clarify some of the "mystery"—the inner meanings and significances—of oriental motifs, and to open new vistas of understanding for the reader who wants to know more about oriental art.

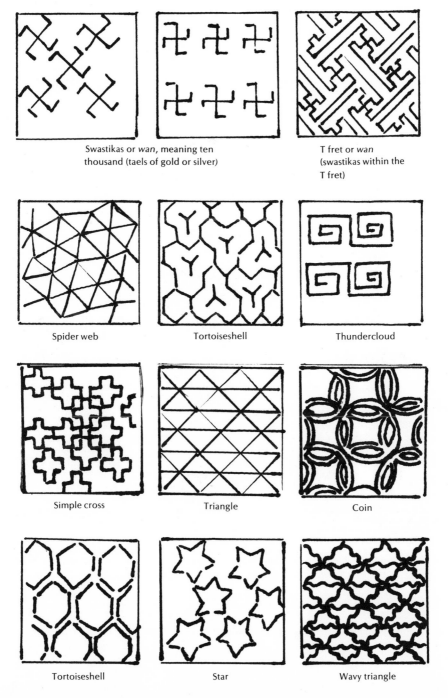

Swastikas or *wan*, meaning ten thousand (taels of gold or silver)

T fret or *wan* (swastikas within the T fret)

Spider web

Tortoiseshell

Thundercloud

Simple cross

Triangle

Coin

Tortoiseshell

Star

Wavy triangle

Fig. 52. Diaper patterns

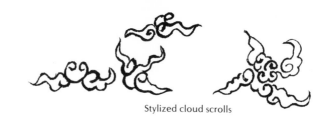

Stylized cloud scrolls

Simplified clouds

Variations of scrolls

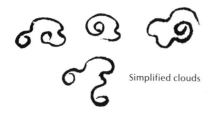

Quatrefoil variations

Lotus stem and leaf

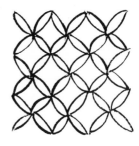

Bud square or rice grain

Waves

Fish scale

Lotus blossom petal

Fig. 53. Additional diaper patterns

10

Repair and Restoration of Cloisonné

WOULDN'T IT BE WONDERFUL IF ART OBJECTS were unbreakable? If all the treasures destroyed each year in fires, floods, and earthquakes were still with us, how much richer man's heritage would be!

The sad truth is that we cannot avoid breaking things. Most art objects are beautiful precisely because they are made of fragile, perishable materials: porcelain, glass, silk, and so on. And if things get damaged, we can only attempt to collect the pieces and try to put them together again. In spite of our best efforts, however, a repaired object is never quite as good as if it had not been broken. Sometimes pieces are missing and we have to fashion replacements. A good repair or restoration job is one that covers damage so that it cannot be easily detected. If a repair cannot be seen with the naked eye, the job can be considered as near-perfect, even perfect.

147

Some collectors believe that broken or damaged objects should never be repaired and/or restored, as a matter of integrity—if a repair is absolutely essential to hold the pieces together, it should be done as conspicuously as possible. There are historical samples to bolster this reasoning. The Chinese used metal staples to hold broken pieces of porcelain together; the Japanese flamboyantly touched up their repair work with gold lacquer. When a dealer gets such items, he will proudly point out the repair as evidence that the piece is "very, very old," and charge you a high price accordingly, even though repairs of this type were made well into the twentieth century.

Today, when all kinds of new products are available to use in making foolproof repairs, there is no need to stick to metal staples and gold lacquer, and few repairmen now employ these obsolete methods. Instead, the essential objective of repair work is to camouflage damage as much as possible. Consider the recent case of Michelangelo's *Pietà*, nearly destroyed by a hammer in the hands of a mentally deranged person. The whole world mourned the disaster, but skilled experts were assembled to restore the masterpiece. When the work was finished, no trace of the damage could be detected.

Through the years, in our search for oriental antiques, we have come upon literally hundreds of cloisonnés with various degrees of damage. Dealers always turn the unsightly damaged part away from the viewer. And browsing customers, as if by intention, invariably turn the bad side toward the front when they leave. After a few weeks of this tug of war, the disgusted dealer is ready to accept any reasonable offer just to get the item off his hands.

Some collectors will not touch damaged pieces at any price, but among such pieces we have often found unusual ones that we like even in their "as is" condition. Finally, with about two hundred of these "eyesores" in our possession, we had to ask ourselves: Can we, having earned the richly deserved but perhaps dubious honor of being the owners of the country's greatest collection of damaged cloisonné, do something to improve its appearance? Certainly showing off our collection in its scarred condition was not adding to our own status as discerning collectors.

It is not easy to find repairmen willing to tackle cloisonné. After years of inquiring, we unearthed just two. Each charged from $40 to $100 per square inch, depending upon how much wire had to be replaced and how difficult the job was. According to our rough estimate, a total of one hundred square inches had to be repaired on the pieces in our collection—an expenditure we could not afford. So we decided to do the repairs ourselves.

We didn't—and we still don't—know how these two repairmen do their work. Theoretically, they can replace the missing wires, fill in glass paste, and fire a piece repeatedly in a kiln at around 850°C to fuse the paste—following the process of cloisonné-making that has been explained in Chapter 3. This would be the ideal way. But to subject a piece—often a valuable and irreplaceable one—to such risk is unthinkable. For one thing, all the enamels would melt and re-fuse and the original colors might change or be ruined. There is no way for even an expert enamelist to avoid such mishaps.

A repairman could use a blowtorch to spot-fuse the filled-in enamels, but even that might do severe damage to adjacent areas, so that the repaired piece could emerge looking more unsightly than before repair was attempted. Incidentally, it might be added that skill in using such a torch is not something a person could develop overnight.

The only alternative to the above procedures is to use substitute materials that can be applied cold. These materials are not real enamels, but synthetic compounds that will cure and harden like enamel.* They will not be as hard as enamel and would be more subject to scratches and wear if the articles were to be used as household utensils. (But who would want to do that anyway?) This modern imitation enamel can be made transparent, translucent, or opaque by adding (or not adding) various powders, such as tin oxide. It can be mixed with colors—dry powdered color, oil base color, watercolor or photo color—to match the original. If the color is not right the first time, it can be scraped off or dug out and redone until it is an exact match. As for missing wires, they can be pressed into the substitute enamel while it is still in a semicured state, or they can be painted on with gold, brass, or copper paint, to simulate the original metal wires.

After we first decided to do our own repairs, we began to visit hobby shops and ask questions. Then we started experimenting on our own. The results of our efforts can be seen in Color Plate 18. All the pieces have been repaired, and the repaired areas are shown facing the reader.

BEFORE ENGAGING IN REPAIR WORK

In our last book, *Oriental Antiques and Collectibles: A Guide*, we devoted a chapter to methods of repairing cloisonné and other types of objects. Many readers tried our process. Here are two rather typical reactions. One lady told us ruefully: "I repaired my cloisonné tea jar, and I made a big mess. But I must admit that I didn't follow your instructions closely." And a dealer friend said: "I had your book before me when I mixed the ingredients and colors. I followed the directions step by step. The result was wonderful. Oh, the first time wasn't truly great, but the second time you couldn't tell the repaired part from the original."

One day we stopped at this dealer's shop and noticed a Chinese cloisonné vase with a red and yellow dragon on a black ground. It was marked $45.

---

*The Chinese cloisonné makers, from earliest times, used to rub hard colored wax on the pieces to cover up holes and blemishes. This process somewhat resembles repairing with imitation enamels applied cold. Perhaps it is not a coincidence that a recent book on cloisonné recommended painting the damaged areas with enamel paint and dripping candle wax into cavities to replace lost enamels!

"That's a reasonable price for such a perfect piece of cloisonné," we remarked.

"Yes, but it's repaired. Here, and here too—you certainly can see that."

"We certainly didn't—at first glance," we assured him.

Now this dealer makes repairing cloisonné a sideline, charging $25 to $50 per piece. He doesn't like to do too much, though. "It isn't difficult work," he says, "but it demands constant attention until each filling is cured. If you walk away from it for as long as two minutes, a repair can turn into a failure."

So we must caution our readers: UNLESS YOU CAN FOLLOW THE INSTRUCTIONS CLOSELY—VERY CLOSELY—DON'T TRY TO REPAIR CLOISONNÉ. FIND SOMEBODY ELSE TO DO IT FOR YOU.

Our second piece of advice: Don't work on your most treasured items until you are reasonably sure you have learned the procedure. Badly damaged ashtrays can be bought for a couple of dollars; practice your repair work on them.

Some damaged pieces are better avoided entirely: 1. Very badly damaged items. They are not worth the time and effort. 2. Articles that have remained in a damaged condition for a long time, so that the damaged areas have become full of dust, grease, patina, and encrustation. It is too difficult to do a thorough cleaning before repair can be done. 3. Poorly and improperly repaired pieces (shun them like the plague). Women, especially, are prone to putting on layer upon layer of nail polish in badly matched colors until a piece is a total disaster. But at a garage sale we saw the man of the house confidently making a last-minute repair by filling a damaged but otherwise beautiful large bowl with a gray sticky substance from a tube labeled "Tailpipe Repair Kit." Telling him to forget the repair, we snatched the item from his hands, to his visible disappointment. We have even found repairs done with concrete!

Without belaboring the point, we must repeat: If an item is badly or improperly repaired, don't bother with it. It is almost impossible to "disrepair" such a piece so that a proper restoration job can be done.

REPAIRS—FROM LIGHT TO HEAVY DAMAGE

Perhaps you knocked over your cloisonné vase while you were cleaning. On the table are some glasslike bits the same color as the peony flower on the vase. Then you notice a damaged area, the size of a dime, on your vase. Obviously the enamel has splintered and a few small pieces have fallen off. Can you get the vase repaired?

This is only superficial damage. The body was not dented; no wire was lost. You don't need to pay a high price to get somebody to make the repair for you. You can do it yourself. You don't even have to know what enamel is or how cloisonné is made. All you need is a little practice, a willingness to follow instructions closely, and a few dollars' investment in some readily available products and coloring agents.

The most necessary item for repairing cloisonné is epoxy glue. When the resin and the hardener come out of the two tubes, they are liquid and transparent; but after thorough mixing they begin to harden into a transparent and solid mass. The hardened cured mixture looks very much like glass. It is not as hard as glass, of course, and it can be sanded into any desired shape. But it is tough and will not crack or break. If this mixture is poured into a cell, it will spread like any other liquid and fill up the cell, attach itself tightly to the base and side walls, and harden into something very much like enamel. When the correct coloring agent is mixed with it, it is an ideal substitute enamel for making proper repairs.

Is repairing really that simple? The answer, unfortunately, is—no. First, you must select an epoxy that is absolutely crystal clear. Most epoxy glues have a yellowish color; with them, you can never make a pure white imitation enamel—it will always be a yellowish white. Nor can you make a true blue; it will always look greenish.

The second necessary quality is that the epoxy should mix with any coloring agent and still cure properly. Many brands refuse to cure if any substance is added to them. So the would-be repairman must first search for the type of epoxy glue he wants, then test its performance before using it in his repair work.

We have tested many different kinds of epoxy products. The one we found most satisfactory is Helor Brand, made by Epoxy Coatings Co., South San Francisco, California 94080. The Master Mending Kit* recently marketed by Atlas is good not only for mending enamel, but also for other repairs, such as those on porcelain and glass. We mention these products purely for the benefit of our readers. We have absolutely no connection with the companies and do not benefit from promoting their products. If, later on, we find a product superior to the above-mentioned brands, we will recommend them in later printings of this book.

MAKING IMITATION ENAMELS

1. Opaque enamels

This is needed for repairing Chinese cloisonné because most Chinese enamels are opaque. First, mix the epoxy glue thoroughly. Then add an opaque coloring agent: powder, tempera, watercolor, poster paint, or oil paint—any one of these will produce good opaque color. The opacity is controlled by the amount of other ingredients added. For black, add fine charcoal dust. For white, add tin oxide. For pastel colors, make the initial color mixture slightly darker than you need, then add tin oxide to lighten. You can improvise in any number of ways. One helpful tip: The fine particles that give opacity to the

---

*Atlas Minerals & Chemicals Division, Mertztown, Pennsylvania 19539.

mixture tend to settle, as in any liquid or semiliquid mixture, leaving the top layer transparent; so it is necessary to stir the mixture constantly until it is semicured, before applying it.

2. Transparent enamels

To make transparent or translucent enamel, select a color agent that does not impart opacity, or at least not too much opacity. Photo colors, for instance, serve the purpose very well. Since they are made to color black-and-white prints, they have to be transparent. The range of colors is extensive, and they are very concentrated—a little goes a long way.

To mix a small quantity of epoxy—which is all one needs—place it on a 2-by-2-inch piece of heavy aluminum foil. (If you are a smoker, save the foil from the cigarette packages. If not, ask your smoker friends to save it for you. It is the best disposable heavy-duty material to mix epoxy on.) Squeeze out equal amounts from each of the two tubes and, with a round toothpick, mix the two ingredients. (Trying to clean utensils is a lost cause; all tools and utensils have to be disposable.)

Another type of epoxy product should also be kept on hand because it can save a great deal of time in repairing deep and extensive damage. This is epoxy putty, a filler that can be manipulated by hand without a messy result. Again, there are many brands on the market. Epoxy putty comes in two sticks —the above-mentioned Atlas kit, for instance, contains it. To use, cut off equal parts from each stick and mix them with fingers. The consistency is somewhat like that of putty, and the material cures and hardens like any other epoxy product. Its greatest advantage is its timesaving quality. You can fill in any space heavily without having the putty run. It is particularly useful when the contour of the body is otherwise impossible to restore or dents are so deep that it would take too many applications to fill them in with the epoxy glue mixture. The proper way to use epoxy putty is not to fill the space all the way to the top. Set two-thirds as the limit, leaving the final one-third to be filled with epoxy glue correctly tinted with the needed color. (If you want to fill to the top, you will then have to sand the surface, paint it over with the correct color, and glaze it thinly with epoxy glue. However, this method is limited to the repair of opaque enamels, such as one finds on Chinese cloisonné; it cannot be used in repairing the transparent or translucent enamels found on most Japanese pieces.)

RESTORING THE CONTOUR

When the body of a cloisonné article has one or more deep dents in it, or if part of the body is bashed in or flattened, you have a choice. You can fill in the damaged areas where the broken enamels have fallen out, or you can restore the shape before applying the imitation enamels. The second procedure is by far the better choice. The shape of wide-mouth or flat items such as trays, bowls, or jars can easily be improved by pressing on the reverse side with your thumbs. During the process, enamels that are already cracked will fall out. Don't worry. They have to come out anyway before a successful restoration can be accomplished.

With a small-necked vase, it is generally impossible to reach the inside through the neck opening. Then it is not only advisable but necessary to remove the base in order to reach the inside of the dented area. This is true of Chinese cloisonné vases. (The bases of Japanese cloisonné vases are usually not detachable. Modern Japanese items, such as those of the popular pigeon blood variety, are often so heavily enameled and counterenameled that any effort to push out a dent may cause further damage. The only way to fill in the damaged area on these is by applying imitation enamels of matching color and translucency.) To remove the base of a vase, put a wooden stick inside the vase through the neck. Push it firmly against the inside of the bottom and tap the stick gently with a hammer. The base will come off, and the inside can then be easily reached. If a heavy accumulation of rust makes a base difficult to detach, use a few drops of a light oil such as "liquid wrench" to soften the rust.

For dents beyond the reach of your fingers, use a wooden spoon or some other round wooden utensil to push the dents out, until the contour of the vase is restored.* (A hammer handle is a good thing to use where neither fingers nor other tools work.) When the body of a piece is of such heavy metal that it is impossible to push out a dented area, you will have to build up the dent on the outside with filler material. (In the case of opaque enamels, use epoxy putty for part of the filling; in the case of translucent or transparent enamels, use epoxy glue mixed with the proper amount of coloring agent, making as many applications as needed.) This process often gives equally satisfactory results, except that the wires, which are often in good shape, will be submerged by the filler material; therefore, if possible, they should first be raised to their original level.

REPLACING WIRES

If the wires are lost or covered by repair material (as mentioned above), they must be replaced. Copper or bronze wires can be bought from hobby shops, and if they are too large in size, the wire can be drawn between a folded sheet of sandpaper until it is reduced to the size needed. Next, the wire must be imbedded in the imitation enamel when it is in a semicured state.

When too much wire has been lost, it is better to wait until the whole process of repair has been finished and then pencil in simulated wires with copper

---

*You may have to file down places that have been pushed too far out.

or bronze paint. They will not look much different from real wires. This type of paint spreads, however, and it is difficult to paint a fake wire as thin as the original; but you can correct your work after the paint is dry by scraping along both sides of the painted wire with a razor blade until the desired width is attained. Or paint over (cover) the unwanted part with colors similar to the surface color(s) adjacent to it.

REPLACING LOST ENAMELS

The most important step in repairing cloisonné is replacing all the lost enamels with imitation enamels of proper color and transparency. We have already explained that enamels have different degrees of transparency, and matching the transparency is as important as matching the original colors. But mixing an imitation enamel of both the desired color and transparency is not an easy job; it takes experience.

Several applications of imitation enamel are necessary to fill in to the desired level—that is, to a slightly higher level than the surrounding area. This "little extra" is needed for the final shaping during which you must scrape or sand a repaired area to exactly the same level and contour as the surrounding surface.

Stir constantly, as you work, to keep the mixed-in color or powder from settling. Again we must remind you that if you fill in too fast, the heavier elements will settle, leaving the top layer transparent. In fact, wait until the mixture is semicured (becomes sticky) before you even start filling in. Of course, at

220. After the dent on this vase was pushed out, the wires were raised and restored to their proper position. Then the damaged area was filled with the recommended material to a level slightly higher than the surrounding surface.

this stage the mixture is still runny, and you must watch the article constantly and tilt it up, down, and sidewise to keep the enamel from running over, spilling out of the dent or well you are filling.

When the imitation enamel has stopped running but before it has hardened, wet your finger and tap it on the mixture. If the enamel does not stick to your finger, you can start shaping it by pressing on the high points and forcing the mixture into places that appear to be low. Keep your finger constantly wet and withdraw it quickly, using a staccato touch. If the mixture sticks to your finger, it is not ready for shaping. Wait a few minutes and try again. Let each application of imitation enamel cure thoroughly before putting on the next one. (The instructions on the product will tell you the approximate curing time.)

Soap and water will remove any of the sticky mixture that adheres to your finger, but nail polish remover (acetone) will do a faster job. It's a good idea to keep a bottle of it on hand along with your repair materials.

When you have completed the last application (having shaped as you went along), you will have achieved a contour only slightly higher than the surrounding area. Now let the epoxy cure at least twenty-four hours before you begin the final shaping. This can be done with a razor blade, by sanding, or by a combination of the two. Often you cannot avoid sanding because it produces a really perfect contour.

Generally speaking, an emery board—use the white side only—serves the purpose very well. Cut the board to any desired shape to suit your needs. You may prefer to use sandpaper, but sometimes some of the grit tends to become embedded in the epoxy; therefore a dark-colored sandpaper can make the repaired part look darker. It is advisable to use light-colored sandpaper only.

Try not to let the sandpaper touch the surrounding area. Put masking tape over any adjoining surface likely to be affected, but when the time comes to

221. After the filler had cured, the patch was sanded down to the desired contour. Note that the wires reappeared.

222. This picture shows how the repaired area looked after it was touched up (within the wires) with colors to match the original. After being given one or two thin coats of clear epoxy, the repair was rubbed down to the desired glossiness. (See also Color Plate 18.)

remove the tape, do not *yank* it off. Old enamels, particularly on a damaged piece, are generally loose or have invisible cracks, and they are easily dislodged. Use a few drops of lighter fluid to loosen the masking tape, and then peel it off slowly and carefully.

If the shaping has been properly completed, you will notice that the wires have reappeared or are at least visible. This is also the time to paint in any missing wires with appropriate metal-toned paint.

The final step is to mix a little clear epoxy and, using your finger, rub a thin coat of it over the repaired area to restore the glossiness. Or you can paint over the repaired area with clear glossy plastic paint. Then let the repaired piece stand for 24 hours. When you examine it again, you probably will find the repaired area much glossier than the surrounding surface. This glossiness can be toned down by gently rubbing the repair with a piece of rough-surfaced cloth. Examine the area frequently while you work. If you have overdone this rubbing so that the repaired area looks too dull, just put on another thin coat of clear epoxy, let it cure, and rub it more gently next time. When the glossiness on your repaired piece appears the same all over the surface, your repair can be deemed a success.

223. Pictured here is a damaged but otherwise most attractive vase. Height 10½ inches; diameter 5½ inches. (See Color Plate 17.)

224. This enlargement shows the extensive damage more clearly. In the bashed-in area, depressed nearly a half inch, all the enamels and wires are gone and the bare copper base shows. The damaged area consists of three-fourths of the design of a chrysanthemum plant having a flower with thin straight petals and green leaves tipped with yellow.

225. To repair this vase, the bottom must first be removed so that you have access to the inside, to push out the dent. At the start, apply a drop of thin oil.

226. After a few minutes, insert a wooden stick through the top and rest it firmly against the base; then hammer the stick-end gently until the bottom falls out.

227. The bottom comes off very easily on most Chinese items.

228. To push out the dent, hold a hammer by the head and gently force the hammer handle along the inside wall of the vase.

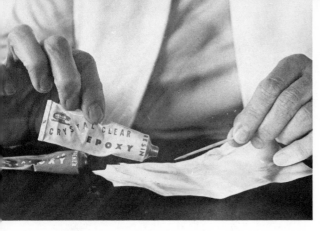

229. Mix epoxy on a piece of heavy foil. Using a round toothpick, mix the two parts according to the manufacturer's directions. (Also see text for instructions on how to make imitation enamels.)

230. A bottle of nail polish remover is a good thing to keep at hand for quick removal of unwanted epoxy mixture.

231. After the mixture has cured, shape the patch by sanding it with the white side of an emery board. Filling and sanding must be repeated several times, until the patch is smooth and just a little below the level of the surrounding area.

232. Cut and shape an emery board into a convenient size for working in small and narrow areas during the shaping operation.

233. So much of the wirework on this vase has been lost that the easier—and perhaps the only—means of restoration is painting in simulated wires with gold, copper, or bronze paint—whichever is closest to the original. Later, if the painted wires appear too thick or uneven, scrape them thin or cover them up with imitation enamel during the next step.

234. Paint the repaired area with appropriate colors to match the original. Then apply one or two coats of clear epoxy. Finally, rub the surface down to the desired glossiness.

235A & B. The finished job. The contour of the vase has been restored to its original shape. The design has also been restored: the straight-petaled flower of white tinged with pink and green is now replaced, and the deep green leaves tipped with yellow have outlines and ribs simulated by wires painted with copperish gold. It can almost pass as an undamaged piece. Unfortunately, the camera lens sometimes sees more than the human eye and sees deeper down, and a black-and-white picture adds a degree of distortion. Therefore, in the photograph the painted wires do not show up as clearly as the original copper wires, which reflect more light; and the area where the green and yellow colors merge into each other appears slightly untidy. (See Color Plate 18.)

OTHER TYPES OF REPAIR WORK

Sometimes a repair cannot be successful without resorting to some type of "surgical technique." For instance, the body of a fine cloisonné vase may be in very good condition, but the neck or foot so badly bashed in that almost all the enamels and wires are gone. Repairing such a piece may require the removal of the entire foot or cutting off a part of the neck.

236. The foot of this vase was crushed out of shape and half broken from the body, and 99 percent of the enamel decoration on the foot was gone. Damage of this extent is impossible to repair.

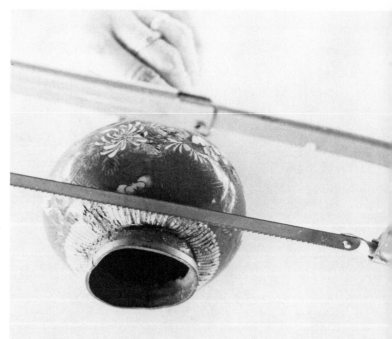

237. The first step was cutting off the foot with a hacksaw.

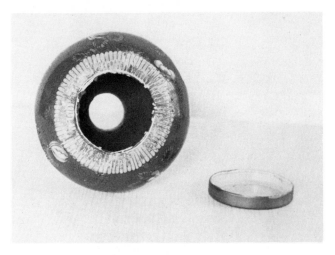

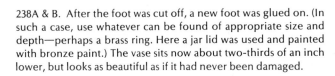

238A & B. After the foot was cut off, a new foot was glued on. (In such a case, use whatever can be found of appropriate size and depth—perhaps a brass ring. Here a jar lid was used and painted with bronze paint.) The vase sits now about two-thirds of an inch lower, but looks as beautiful as if it had never been damaged.

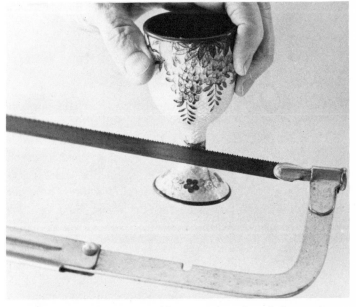

239. This delicate stem cup with translucent enamels was so bent by a fall that it no longer stood up straight.

240. Since it was almost impossible to straighten this tubular metal stem without losing—unwarrantedly—a great deal more of the damaged enamels, we cut the stem almost halfway through at the point of the bend.

241. The stem was then easy to straighten.

242. After filling in the stem, a silver coating was applied, then several coats of clear, light bluish green imitation enamel. (See Color Plate 18.)

After you have learned how to repair cloisonné, you will find repairing champlevé a very simple matter: just fill in the cells with imitation enamels of the appropriate colors. There are no missing wires to worry about because the cells or cavities will always remain in good condition.

Repairing damaged painted enamel wares is also relatively simple: first, fill in the background, which is often white. If the background happens to be in color, you had better fill that in last. Next, pencil in the design, following the original as nearly as possible, although you can add a leaf here, a rock there, to hide a badly damaged spot. Use Chinese (black) ink and a Chinese brush to do the job. But of course any tool (a fine-tipped felt pen, for example) that can achieve the same results will do equally well.

Finally, fill in the design with imitation enamels or appropriate colors. After all the work has been satisfactorily done, you can rub on a thin coat of clear epoxy to give the whole piece an overall glossiness.

243. A damaged but otherwise exquisitely painted enamel piece. Diameter 7½ inches.

244. The same plate after repair.

MAKING DECORATIVE ITEMS FROM DAMAGED CLOISONNÉ

In China they have long said: "If you find potsherds of Chai ware [a porcelain made in the tenth century, and now nonexistent], don't throw them away. Use them to make hat ornaments, belt decorations, or trinkets, for they are extremely valuable." The same can be said of many other kinds of antiques. If you happen to have cloisonné items damaged beyond repair, they can still be cut, sanded, and made into decorative ornaments.

The process is simple. From a damaged vase, bowl, or plate, select the part of the design that is still in good condition. Outline this part with a thin line of clear epoxy. Or, to be safer still, coat the whole object with clear epoxy. Likewise, coat the underside. This epoxy coating will hold the enamels and wires in place and keep them from breaking when you start cutting.

Next, get a hard saw blade such as one of tungsten steel. (A fine-toothed hacksaw blade will do.) Gently saw along the outside of the epoxy-outlined or coated area. Do not use too much pressure, and *never* use a metal cutter or shears. When the piece is cut loose, you can shape it with sanding. Again, work gently and do not use much pressure.

After the piece has been shaped, paint the edge with metal paint, or mix epoxy with copper powder and form a rim around it. The powder (gold, bronze, copper, silver) can be bought at any hobby shop. Of course if you are good at metalwork, you can make a real copper or silver rim for your creation. Now you have a cloisonné plaque that can be glued to a small bronze box, made into a necklace pendant, or set into a bracelet or ring. You will be proud of your ingenuity!

But do not attempt to make expensive snuff bottles out of cheap salt and pepper shakers even if you can make them functional. (And we must admit that we have seen many snuff bottles that are hardly functional.) However, now and then we have noticed clever conversions—the perforated top had been replaced by a glass cap (Peking glass, of course!) with a tiny spoon attached to it. The concept is ingenious. But the thing is an outrage!

245. This was the top of a cosmetic box that was beyond repair. The solder along the rim was removed with sandpaper. Then, using epoxy glue, two rings were attached through which cord could be strung. Now it serves as an elegant pendant, 3 inches in diameter.

246. After the guests left, you found one of your treasured cloisonné napkin rings on the floor, sadly flattened, with enamel splinters all around it. Well, don't blame your favorite uncle, the inveterate napkin ring stepper-on-er. You may have lost a napkin ring, but you have gained a pendant if you just use your repair knowledge and ingenuity.

247. Even a cut-out from a broken ashtray can be fitted onto a necklace.

248. An old lamp finial, crushed at both ends because the lamp owner liked a finial to be extra secure and very tight. Hide the damage with two large Peking glass beads fitted snugly into the depressions. Attach it to a cord and, voilà! you have a pendant sure to become a conversation piece.

Price Guide

As MENTIONED BEFORE, an accurate and specific price list, in the opinion of the authors, is scarcely feasible. In this book, we had hoped to get by without one, but the gentle persuasion of both our publisher and our readers was hard to resist. However, this guide must be interpreted with the utmost latitude. Above all, when buying antiques or collectibles, the buyer should first consider the artistic quality of the piece. Next, the workmanship and the condition of the item should be examined before consulting this or any other price guide.

It must be said that any specimen having the status of "antique," meaning over one hundred years old, should always be appraised by a knowledgeable expert. The risk involved, in terms of dollars spent, is usually very high.

This list, therefore, can cover only items of the "collectible" category—that is, things that are still readily available on the market. Not all items listed here were mentioned or illustrated in the text, but they are available and so have been included.

BOXES (Cloisonné)

Rectangular or square, with or without hinges, size approximately 2 by 2 by 4 inches; or round, 2 inches-3 inches in diameter; Chinese: $25-$50. (Japanese boxes often have unusual shapes and exquisite workmanship; prices can be much higher.)

Chinese matchbox holders and ashtrays: $8-$15.

Japanese match safes (usually hinged and of good workmanship): $25 and up.

Cigarette boxes, cylindrical, with flat or domed tops:
    Chinese: $20-$25.
    Japanese (usually of the pigeon-blood variety with rose bouquet design): $15-$20.

VASES (Cloisonné)

Chinese, 6-9 inches; ca. 1900-1935: $50-$100. 10-20 inches: $75-$250 and up.

Japanese, traditional and/or naturalistic, 5-9 inches: $45-$125. 10-20 inches: $100-$275 and up.

Japanese, including recent imports: 6-9 inches: $70-$100.

Japanese, transparent enamel over foil, 3-6 inches: $20-$50 and up.

Plique-à-jour vases or bowls of early (ca. 1900) or recent make: $200 and up.

JARS (Cloisonné)

Tea jars, including potiches:
    Chinese; 6-8 inches in diameter: $75-$125.
    Japanese, traditional designs (covered, sectional or not; gold-flecked or not); 6-9 inches in diameter: $85-$150 and up.

Jardinieres (usually Japanese), 12 inches in diameter: $200 and up.

PLATES (Cloisonné)

Chinese, 12 inches in diameter (rather unusual, often quite old): $225 and up.

Japanese, 12 inches in diameter, naturalistic designs: $225 and up.

BOWLS (Cloisonné)

Rice bowls (usually Chinese): $15-$35.
Flat bowls (of bulb-bowl type), Chinese or Japanese, decorated inside and out;
7-9 inches in diameter: $85-$150 and up.

TRAYS (Cloisonné)

Pin or card—Chinese or Japanese; diameter 2-4 inches: $10-$20.
Serving—Chinese or Japanese; length 5-9 inches: $35 and up.

MISCELLANEOUS CLOISONNÉ ITEMS

Beads or earrings, Chinese or Japanese (including recently made items): $6-
$15.
Napkin rings: $8-$10.
Wine cups: $3-$10.
Steins: $35 and up.
Miniature pitchers, teapots, tea jars; also salt and pepper sets: $18 and up.

WINE POTS (Cloisonné)

Wine pots or ewers, of different shapes, forms, and sizes—Chinese or Japanese; approximately 4-6 inches in height: $120-$250.

SNUFF BOTTLES (Cloisonné)

To be judged on beauty and quality only. Most on the market were never
used; many were made recently, but the workmanship is good to excellent:
$85 and up.

FIGURAL SPECIMENS IN CLOISONNÉ

Among the more expensive items are human and animal figures in the
round, which first attained popularity during the Ch'ien-lung period; they
were also produced during the subsequent years and are even now made in
China. Sometimes, it is difficult to tell whether a piece is of the Ch'ien-lung
period or only in the style thereof. Also in the expensive category are odd and
rare items such as moon-flasks and all those things that inspire the comment:
"I've never seen anything like this before," or "I'll be darned!" They, of
course, must be appraised by an expert who knows the market conditions.

CHAMPLEVÉ OBJECTS

Japanese champlevé objects of good quality—that is, those of smooth cast-bronze work, and antiqued by lacquering—are often handsome, large, heavy pieces worth $100 or more each. (The lacquer on older pieces may be worn off because of constant use, or it may be prematurely "lost" through the efforts of Westerners, who like their "bronzes" shiny and bright.) Rough, brassy champlevé objects haphazardly filled with enamels are not worth very much.

SPECIAL ITEMS (Cloisonné)

Japanese cloisonné on pottery or cloisonné in lacquer objects can be considered unique and rare, or merely as specimens to round out a collection. The worth of such items is a consideration that only the buyer (in the last analysis) can determine.

NEW CLOISONNÉ IMPORTS

Recent imports from China are available in almost all the listed categories, from elaborately decorated vases and human and animal figures down to snuff bottles, beads, and—yes—even napkin rings! They command prices equal to or higher than pre-World War II items. These new objects are very decorative and of excellent workmanship. Although most of the designs are traditional, there are some innovations. The color range has been expanded somewhat—in particular, to include several shades of bright orange that were not used prior to the establishment of the present government.

Japanese pieces recently exported to the United States are heavy and of good quality. Those from the Inaba Company are of a quality that commands deservedly high prices.

CHINESE PAINTED ENAMEL

Items of exceptionally good quality and painting are equal in value to cloisonné items of comparative size and condition. Such fine pieces are rare, however; as a rule, painted enamels are worth a quarter to a third less than cloisonné. Transparent and translucent enamels over stamped repoussé designs are worth even less than comparable pieces in painted ware. These pieces were attractive when new, but the enamels were applied thinly. Very few are found in good condition, and so one cannot estimate their value with any accuracy.

Bibliography

AMIRANASHRILI, SHALVA. *Medieval Georgian Enamels of Russia.* New York: Harry Abrams, Inc., 1960.

ASHTON, LEIGH, AND GRAY, BASIL. *Chinese Art.* New York: The Beechurst Press, 1953.

BARSALI, ISA BELLI. *European Enamels.* London, New York, Sydney, Toronto: Paul Hamlyn, 1966 & 1969.

BOWES, JAMES L. *Japanese Enamels.* Liverpool. (Printed for private circulation 1884.)

————. *Notes on Shippo.* London: Paternoster House, Charing Cross Rd., Kegan Paul, Trench, Trubnes & Co. Ltd., 1895.

BURLING, JUDITH AND ARTHUR. *Chinese Art.* New York: Bonanza Books, 1953.

BUSHELL, RAYMOND. *Chinese Arts,* vols. 1 and 2. London: Victoria and Albert Museum, published under the authority of the Board of Education, 1924.

172

CHRISTIE, ANTHONY. *Chinese Mythology.* London, New York, Sydney, Toronto: Paul Hamlyn, 1968.

CHU, ARTHUR AND GRACE. *Oriental Antiques and Collectibles, A Guide.* New York: Crown Publishers, 1973.

CLARKE, GEOFFREY, AND FEHER, FRANCIS & IDA. *The Technique of Enameling.* New York: Reinhold, 1967.

DAVID, SIR PERCIVAL. *Chinese Connoisseurship,—The Ko Ku Yao Lun, The Essential Criteria of Antiquities.* (With a facsimile of the Chinese text of 1388.) London: Faber and Faber, 1971.

DE KONINGH, H. *The Preparation of Precious and Other Metal Work for Enamelling.* New York: The Norman W. Henley Publishing Co., 1930.

GARNER, SIR HARRY. *Chinese and Japanese Cloisonné Enamels.* London: Faber & Faber, 1962 (revised edition 1970).*

GETZ, JOHN. *Catalogue of the Avery Collection of Ancient Chinese Cloisonnés.* Museum of the Brooklyn Institute of Arts and Sciences. Brooklyn, New York: The De Vinne Press, 1912.

GORHAM, HAZEL H. *Japanese and Oriental Ceramics.* Rutland, Vermont, and Tokyo, Japan: Charles E. Tuttle Co., 1971.

JOURDAIN, MARGARET, AND JENYNS, R. SOAME. *Chinese Export Art in the Eighteenth Century.* London: Spring Books, 1950.

KYUSABURO, KAIYAMA. (Translation by Sylvia Price Mueller.) *The Book of Japanese Design.* New York: Crown Publishers, 1969.

National Palace Museum. *Masterpieces of Chinese Enamel Ware.* Taipei, Taiwan: National Palace Museum, 1971.

NEWBLE, BRIAN. *Practical Enameling and Jewelry Work.* A Studio Book. New York: The Viking Press, 1967.

OGITA, TOMOO, AND PETTERSON, RICHARD. Unedited, limited edition of *Asian Cloisonné Enamels from the Dorothy Adler Routh Museum.* Claremont, Calif.: Claremont College Print Shop, 1974.

SNOWMAN, A. KENNETH. *The Art of Carl Fabergé.* London: Faber & Faber Ltd., 1953.

UNTRACHT, OPPI. *Enameling on Metal.* Phila., Pa.: Chilton Co., 1959.

MAGAZINES AND PERIODICALS

BLUETT, EDGAR. "Chinese Cloisonné in the Krolik Collection." *Oriental Art*, vol. XI, 1965.

CHAIT, R. M. "Dating Early Chinese Enamels." *Oriental Art*, Vol. III, Nov. 1950.

*Scholarly treatise on the subject of cloisonné enamels, a must reading for serious collectors.

"Collector." "Chinese Cloisonné, The Robert and Marian Clague Collection." *Arts of Asia*, January-February 1975.

HOBSON, R. L. "On Chinese Cloisonné Enamel." *Burlington Magazine*, vol. XXI, April-Sept. 1912.

————."A Note on Canton Enamels." *Burlington Magazine*, vol. XXII, Dec. 1912.

JENYNS, R. SOAME. "Chinese Art—The Minor Arts, Cloisonné." *Universe*, New York: 1963.

————."The Problem of Chinese Cloisonné Enamels." *Transactions of Oriental Ceramic Society*, London: 1949.

LEARY, R. H. "Cloisonné." *Arts of Asia*, May-June 1973.

————."Cloisonné: The Ching T'ai Myth." *Arts of Asia*,* January-February 1975.

NGUYET, TUYET, AND LEARY, R. H. "Inaba Cloisonné." *Arts of Asia*,* September-October 1973.

SIMMONS, PAULINE. "Chinese Cloisonné Enamels." *Bulletin of the Metropolitan Museum of Art*, vol. XXIV, #9.

YUAN, TE-HSING. "Conceptions of Painting in the Shang and Shou Dynasties" (a description and discussion of designs on ancient Chinese bronze vessels), Parts I & II. *National Palace Museum Bulletins*. Vols. IX and X, May-June, July-August 1974.

*Article of particular significance on the subject.

Index

Page numbers in italics refer to illustrations.